Sure it was all in the newspapers. So was Pearl Harbor and World War II and so many other widely-chronicalled events. But they still write books about them. That's what history's about and that's what this book is—a history of a crazed gunman who turned New York into a terror-stricken city for more than a year.

GEORGE CARPOZI JR.

SON OF SAM

THE .44-CALIBER KILLER

GEORGE CARPOZI JR.

MANOR BOOKS INC.

A MANOR BOOK 1977

Manor Books, Inc.
432 Park Avenue South
New York, N. Y. 10016

Published by arrangement with the author.
Printed in the United States

ISBN CODE 0-532-22112-5

Other Books by George Carpozi Jr.

CONTENTS

Book II Son of Sam's Own Story

Book III After the Fact

Photo Section Follows Page 192

THE INNOCENTS...
THE MURDERED
AND THE MAIMED

DONNA LAURIA—She wasn't a glamour freak but she enjoyed dressing up. She was a living doll. She was teased by her brothers a good deal of the time because they loved her so. She died in her eighteenth year of life, the first victim of the .44-caliber killer.

JODY VALENTE—Donna's best friend who was with her the night New York City's most depraved killer struck, was shot in the left thigh. The memory of that horrendous experience will live with this 19-year-old girl forever.

JOANNE LOMINO, an 18-year-old beauty, was in the dumps because she'd just been laid off from work. Then the .44-caliber killer pulled the trigger and the bullet lodged in her spine. Unemployment will not concern Joanne again. She was paralyzed by the slug that plowed into her back.

Joanne's friend, 16-year-old DONNA DE-MASI, is lucky to be alive and fortunate to have suffered a mere fracture of her collar-bone. Donna is thankful that she escaped with her life when gunned down in the mad killer's second onslaught.

Twenty-six-year-old CHRISTINE FREUND was looking forward eagerly to the announcement of her engagement to John Diel on St. Valentine's Day. She was in her beau's car, parked and necking. The .44-caliber killer's bullet ended her dream—and her life.

CARL DENARO and his date had an appointment with friends following a Friday night outing with his girlfriend. They drove into a parking lot and just as they were to leave the car and go to their rendezvous it happened. All at once Denaro felt a "ping" in his head and heard a crashing sound. The .44-caliber killer, mistaking long-haired Denaro for a girl, triggered the shot at him.

She had a glowing future as a language teacher, this 19-year-old daughter of Armenian immigrant parents. VIRGINIA VOSKER-ICHIAN was in her sophomore year at Columbia University, studying languages, when the psychopathic gunman fired a .44-caliber bullet into her mouth and killed her instantly.

VALENTINA SURIANI was only eighteen but her life also ended too soon when shot in the head by the madman who surprised her and the young man she planned to marry in the near future.

He held on for life just a little longer than his sweetheart, but 20-year-old ALEXANDER ESAU underwent surgery after the bullet from the killer's gun entered his head and he died eighteen hours later. He was the fifth fatality of the night marauder's frightful rampages.

JUDY PLACIDO came from the Bronx. A 17-year-old, she was full of vim and vigor. Then, after a night of revelry at a Queens discotheque enjoying some reverie with a date in a car, suddenly her forehead, neck, and temple were dripping blood. Son of Sam had struck once more.

The frightening flash of exploding light, the crash of glass, and the sting of excruciating pain doesn't elude Judy's beau, SALVA-

TORE LUPO. This 20-year-old mechanic's helper is wounded in two parts of his body, but like Judy he hasn't suffered serious injury.

STACY MOSKOWITZ' ex-fiance had warned her to be wary of the .44-caliber killer. But his 20-year-old girlfriend poo-pooed the threat. Stacy was a blonde and she felt safe because *he* went after young people with long, dark hair. Stacy's life was snuffed out by one of the last bullets Son of Sam fired.

Her date, ROBERT VIOLANTE, also 20, survived the attack but he may never see again. The bullet that tore through his head destroyed his right eye and apparently caused permanent damage to his left.

These are the victims. What follows is the story of how they and many others became the innocent sufferers in the year-long rampage of a killer who stalked the streets of New York City with a dread Wild West-type .44-caliber revolver and shot at helpless young people wherever he found them...

A DIARY OF KILLING AND CRIPPLING

BOOK ONE

CHAPTER I

ASSASSINATING BY THE NUMBERS

New York City.

The Big Apple.

A metropolis gripped by palpable fear!

It wasn't the financial crisis and the constant, unrelenting threat of bankruptcy which terrified New York but the ominous and awesome presence of an apparently psychopathic gunman.

The .44-caliber killer!

Though not the first time in the city's history that a murderous assassin had gone on a death-dealing rampage, it certainly was the first instance when a gunman zeroed in on a particular type of victim by the numbers— women with brown, shoulder-length hair. Repeatedly and almost without variation.

The .44-caliber killer's litany of murders is now over. The alleged killer was captured finally and at last after more than a year of bloody marauding that added up to eight harrowing nighttime attacks in quiet, residential, crime-free neighborhoods which left a final toll of six young people dead and seven others who suffered various degrees of wounds.

The figures are not terrifyingly large in contrast to tolls compiled by history's rogue's gallery of compulsive mass murderers who've written their legacies in the blood of their many innocent, unsuspecting, and helpless victims.

Yet his outrages against society are significant and, indeed, unique.

For never in New York City's long and lustrous history had there ever been a criminal rampage of this sort.

The nearest comparable reign of terror of such magnitude was the frightening escapades of the notorious Mad Bomber in the 1940s and 1950s.

In more recent times there'd been terroristic bombings by Puerto Rican nationalists seeking independence for their island commonwealth, as well as isolated cases of other violent demonstrations for causes which employed explosives to kill, to maim and to spread fear.

But the case of George Metesky, which lasted for a generation and ended a generation ago with his arrest, is perhaps the only comparable case in New York City's history in which a nihilist committed repeated and haphazard outrages without ever spelling out the grievances which precipitated his acts of violence.

Yet upon history's broad and undulating panorama, New York's own experiences with the madmen of those varied eras is but a mere sprinkle on the world landscape of coldly-calculated killings.

For there have been countless cases of mass

murderers acting out their murky motives through bizarre patterns of death throughout the world...

Perhaps the most infamous of those killers was Jack The Ripper, also known as Saucy Jack and Leather Apron.

The preserve for dispensing his heinous outrages against human life was London's dreary East End in 1888 when he is said to have slashed to death at least five prostitutes—and very possibly as many as fourteen.

Scotland Yard struggled for years to establish a motive for this murderer's madnesses, but never reached a resolution. Perhaps the closest inkling of a motive came in a letter from the purported killer to the news agency Reuters.

"I am down on whores," he wrote. "And I shan't quit ripping them..."

Jack The Ripper was never tracked nor taken.

In more recent times, the world has experienced many acts of terrorism, but none matched the political massacre of 1972 when savage Palestinian commandos killed eleven Israeli Olympic competitors at the XX Olympiad on September 5, 1972, in Munich.

That ignominious day of terror began at 4:30 a.m. when a Palestinian commando squad scaled a wall in the Olympic Village and forced their way into the quarters of the Israeli Olympic team.

Moshe Weinberg, the wrestling coach, and

Joseph Romano, a weightlifter, resisted and were shot to death. Nine other Israelis were held hostage while West German authorities surrounded the building.

The terrorists demanded release of two-hundred Arabs held in Israeli prisons, and an airplane to fly them to a safe port of call.

They were provided with a Boeing 727 jetliner which they expected would fly them with their hostages to the Middle East. Instead, West German sharpshooters fired on them. One Arab hurled a grenade that killed some Israeli hostages and soon after the 20-hour reign of terror was over.

The final toll was 11 Israelis, one Munich policeman, and five Arab guerrillas slain.

Back in the United States, there have been many mass murders in recent times, committed both by renegades with a cause and killers with no apparent motive to justify their acts.

In 1960, Ronald York and James Latham, teenaged soldiers confined to the disciplinary barracks at Fort Hood in Texas, decided to embark on a bone-chilling rampage of murder.

They discarded their Army clothes, strolled out of the stockade, and embarked on a terrifying cross-country murder spree which cost seven lives.

Following their capture, York rationalized:

"Those we killed are all better off dead and out of this rat race ..."

In 1965, some five years after their murderous rampage, Ronald York and James Latham paid for their crime.

They were hanged!

Then there was Chicago's "Crime of the Century."

It happened on July 14, 1966.

Never before in Chicago's violent history—not even in its gangland heyday of the Roaring Twenties—had mass murder been committed on such a scale. Nothing before it quite equalled the horror and shock that came with the slayings of eight young student nurses.

Only once before in that city had there been anything even remotely so terrible in the butchery of human lives—the 1929 St. Valentine's Day massacre when seven men were lined up facing the brick wall of a garage on Clark Street and riddled to death by four underworld executioners wielding shotguns and machine guns. The assassinations stemmed from a bitter feud between gangster Bugs Moran, the victims' boss, and the infamous Al Capone.

That record stood for twenty years, until September 6, 1949, when Howard B. Unruh, a seemingly mild, 28-year-old World War II veteran, took a twenty-minute stroll through his Camden, N. J. neighborhood with his war souvenir Luger pistol, firing at everyone he saw.

The carnage he wrought added up to thirteen human lives.

Nine years later, in 1959, 19-year-old Charles Starkweather embarked on a 525-mile trip from Lincoln, Nebraska, to Douglas, Wyoming, with a kidnapped 14-year-old girl by his side. In a 48-hour period he slaughtered ten people.

On that morning of July 14, 1966, America was awakening to reports on the progress of preparations for the launch of Astronauts John Young and Michael Collins aboard Gemini 10 for a space ride that would bring them to a rendezvous with an Atlas-Agena rocket target vehicle.

A tropical storm had been threatening to force a postponement of the blastoff from Cape Kennedy, but then skies cleared and the spacemen got the happy word "go" for their three-day journey into space.

But suddenly at that very moment the clatter of the wire service teletypewriters in newspaper offices across America turned their attention to another part of the country.

To Chicago.

Instantly, the headlines "Gemini Pair Get The Go-Go" were replated to read: "Eight Student Nurses Slain In Chicago."

Richard Speck, the man who committed that orgy of mass slaughter on a scale never witnessed before or since in Chicago, beat the chair after a trial. But for whatever consolation it may be to the scores of sleuths who toiled to avenge the savage murders of the eight young women, Richard Speck was at least permanently removed from society when his death sentence was commuted to life imprisonment.

The narrative of *assassinating by the numbers* continued into the spring of 1971 when the California police uncovered the bodies of twenty-five men buried in peach orchards outside Yuba City.

All the victims were found to be derelicts and hoboes. They had all been hacked and stabbed to death.

Juan V. Corona, a farm labor contractor, was arrested after a long and tedious investigation by authorities. Then throughout the many months of his trial, the prosecution piled up incontrovertible evidence that linked the defendant to the murders.

Nevertheless, a motive was never proffered to the jury.

Corona's lawyer challenged the State's charge against his client, contending that the real killer wasn't Corona but a homosexual who had paid the derelicts and hoboes for sexual favors before killing them.

The jury deliberated long and hard. They came back with a verdict leaving no doubt they believed the prosecution. Juan Corona was found guilty and sentenced to twenty-five life terms in prison.

Then there's that baffling and still-unsolved West Coast case of Ted, the Seattle Slayer, whose modus operandi has elements similar to those of the .44-caliber killer. But the differences are more pronounced.

It was in 1974 when six strikingly similar

21

and attractive young women vanished in the Seattle area. The only clue authorities dredged up on the disappearances was a slender thread that seemed to tie each of the missing women to a young, handsome man who approached them on the beach at various times during that Summer.

He called himself Ted and, according to the skimpy evidence investigators developed, he invariably approached the girls with his arm in a sling, soliciting their hand to hitch a sailboat to his car.

Abduction and murder apparently followed. Apparently because none of the victims—all strikingly similar in appearance and build, all attractive young women—has been found. And so far no motive has been established.

Another apparently psychotic, compulsive killer with a fixation to harm skid row bums was Vaughn Greenwood, known as the *Los Angeles Slasher*. The 33-year-old drifter was sentenced to life imprisonment in 1976 for the murders of eleven men.

Greenwood apparently followed a strange ritual in each of his cold-blooded knife killings:

Finding his victims asleep or drunk, Greenwood arranged the bodies with considerable care so they were positioned to his satisfaction. After removing the shoes and placing them beside the body, Greenwood slashed the victim's throat from ear to ear.

Then he filled a cup of blood from the

throbbing jugular of the dying man and deposited it on the ground beside the corpse.

Like so many others in the rogue's gallery of compulsive killers, no motive for the killings was ever offered.

But is it necessary to have a motive?

If one is indeed in that class of genuinely compulsive or psychotic killers, then he need not have a rational motive as it has come to be understood in the conventional sense.

He's a special class of criminal. He:

Doesn't want money or valuables or drugs or public recognition...

Won't take hostages...

Will not kill for any of the conventional reasons...

Seldom leaves clues or evidence that will help police pick up his trail of death...

As a consequence of that weird and irregular pattern of murder and the attendant cleverly-executed coverup, authorities are compelled to search out otherwise insignificant and usually ignored signs, characteristics, and actions of each victim to help develop leads to the killer.

These signs, characteristics, and actions are known as "stimuli."

Or as Dr. Emanuel F. Hammer, a leading forensic psychologist and former director of the Psychological Section of New York County Criminal Court put it: "The common denominator is that the victim must be a symbolic representation very vital and important to the killer's life."

23

It could be something as simple and seemingly insignificant as the color of someone's hair which can turn that person into a symbol for the killer passing by. Every one of the .44-caliber killer's victims, except one, had long, dark hair—four of the five young women he killed and the six he maimed. And even the young man he murdered and the one he wounded had worn their dark hair long!

Yet hair color, or its length, may not have been the triggering factor in the killings at all. For very often it's been shown after a compulsive killer was arrested, his statement—even confession—shed little or no light on the motive for murder.

Most often, the reasons are buried in the deepest recesses of the killer's psyche. And no amount of probing by forensic alienists can dig out the answers.

In studying the modus operandi of the .44-caliber killer, Dr. Hammer also saw another possible *stimulus*: "In three of the killings, the victims were shot in the company of male companions," he observed. "I believe the victim could have represented women who had rejected the killer in the past.

"Perhaps, too, the victims were taking the place of a mother who was most rejecting of the killer when she was in the same age range as the victim.

"Or—both figures may pertain. The current rejection by a young woman of the killer's advances may touch upon a raw wound of earlier, maternal rejection."

But at the same time, Dr. Hammer warned, the annihilation of the symbolic victim would not necessarily assuage the killer's fury nor thirst to take lives.

One of the classic examples of that concept was the New Jersey case of Howard Unruh who ran amok on the streets of Camden, gunning down pedestrians at will. By the time he was captured, he had killed thirteen. Unruh had vented his frustration on the populace because he had wanted to kill his mother—but was unable to.

Dr. Hammer, who examined Unruh, noted: "If he had connected and killed his mother, there would have been only one murder..."

And that raised new questions at the time about the .44-caliber killer:

When would New York City's psychopathic killer feel assuaged?

Or would the killings go on and on until the assassin was captured or shot down himself?

For more than a year the answers to those questions eluded the 28,000 policemen searching the endless miles of New York City's streets and sidewalks for that madman.

No one but the .44-caliber killer could really know where or when he was going to strike again.

And that's what made his very existence so terrifying...

CHAPTER II

IN THE BEGINNING...

July 29, 1976
A warm, moonlit night, a Thursday.
The time was 1:10 a.m.

A vivacious dark-haired girl, her tresses falling in a pleasant flow to her slender shoulders, sat easily in the parked car chatting animatedly with her pretty brunette companion who also wore her neatly-coiffed hair in a long, sweeping style.

Eighteen-year-old Donna Lauria occupied the passenger side of the front seat nearest the sidewalk and nineteen-year-old Jody Valente was behind the steering wheel of her 1975 blue Oldsmobile that was double-parked outside the six-story yellow brick building at 2860 Buhre Avenue, a quiet, tree-lined street which looked more like a neighborhood in the suburbs than a residential section of New York City.

The locale was just three blocks from the southern perimeter of Pelham Bay Park, one of the few expanses of verdant greenland in the Bronx and less than two-thirds of a mile from the craggy shore of Eastchester Bay. The neighborhood itself had not yet been contaminated by the rapid spread of the festering blight afflicting so many of the borough's other residential and business communities being transformed into burned-out, uninhabitable ghettos by a populace mistakenly referred to as "animals," when in truth they are much worse. Savages is a much more appropriate term for these people with the mien, disposition, temperament, and mentality of barbaric annihilators of civilization's dignities and values.

So caught up were Jody and Donna in their free-flowing, easy-paced, carefree banter that they barely heard the call from the sidewalk.

"Hi, Donna... Hi, Jody," the voice greeted.

At that moment Donna had been telling Jody about a funny incident that had happened to her the day before at her job as an emergency medical technician for a private hospital ambulance service in Manhattan.

"I don't even remember what it was about anymore," Jody was to say at a later time. "What happened in the next instant shattered my memory of the story Donna was telling— shattered it totally and completely."

The girls had just returned from a night out. They had met a couple of hours earlier following a date Donna had with her twenty-one-year-old fiance, Stanley Wisniewski, who worked as a paramedic with Donna for the Empire State Ambulance Service at New York Hospital.

At the sound of their names, the girls turned and looked toward the sidewalk.

"Hello, Mom," Donna called out. "Hi, Dad..."

Rose and Michael Lauria were just returning themselves from an evening out when they spotted their daughter and her friend.

"Coming up soon?" asked Mrs. Lauria in a cheerful voice.

"Be up in a minute, Mom," Donna promised.

The parents reached the front door and Lauria was pressing the thumb latch when they heard the door of the double-parked car open and shut. Donna had gotten out and begun walking up behind her parents.

But then all at once she stopped, whirled around, and hurried back to the car.

"What was that about?" Lauria asked his wife as the couple entered the foyer.

"She probably remembered something she wanted to tell Jody," Mrs. Lauria suggested in a response that could only have come from a mother who understood the working of her daughter's mind.

Looking out the front entrance, Lauria observed his daughter getting back into the car and closing the door.

The couple went up to their apartment on the fourth floor where their other two children, nineteen-year-old Michael and fourteen-year-old Louis, were asleep.

As they closed the door and made their way through the apartment to the master bedroom, Lauria and his wife were startled by a series of loud explosions from the street. At first they imagined it was the backfire of a car. But then they suspected the worst when they heard a feminine voice crying out shrilly.

They hurried to a window overlooking the street and were terrified by the scene.

There was Jody Valente struggling out of the car and then limping in the middle of the roadway in what seemed like an aimless back and forth jaunt of the street.

"Help me! Help me!" she was screaming.

The Laurias didn't wait to see anymore. They shouted to their sons, who by now were out of bed, and they all rushed downstairs to the street.

Meanwhile, Jody's outcries awakened many residents in this predominantly Irish and Italian neighborhood and they gaped with inordinate curiosity and bewilderment from their open windows.

They were able to see now what the Lauria's couldn't see from inside the stairwell they were descending at this very instant. Jody had finally returned from her inexplicable middle-of-the-street zigzagging and hobbled in a straight, direct path finally to the other side of the car where Donna had been sitting.

Crying out, "Donna! Donna!" Jody opened the car door and her girlfriend toppled limply out of the front seat. Her body fell like a weighted sack, head first out of the car and struck the pavement with a sickening thud.

As the onlookers from on high gasped in horror, Jody exploded anew with anguished screams.

Just then the Laurias burst out of the apartment building. The sight of their daughter's unmoving body sprawled on the street beside the car generated cacaphonous, hysterical outbursts by the family.

Her parents and brothers knelt beside Donna in a desperate but futile attempt to minister to her. Then they quickly sensed the utter uselessness of their efforts.

From the large flow of blood from the back of the head, it was obvious even to those nearest and dearest to her that there was nothing they could do for Donna. Even if Jody Valente was not broken up and weeping uncontrollably—and not bleeding from the left thigh—she still could not have been expected to apply any lesson she'd been taught up to then as a nurse in training.

She couldn't have helped her friend.

There wasn't anything anyone could do for Donna Lauria now...

It was up to the ambulance doctor from Jacobi Hospital to make it official by pronouncing the victim D.O.A.—dead on arrival.

Jody, who'd been shot in the left thigh and was bleeding profusely, was given emergency first aid at the scene, then taken to the hospital. Her condition wasn't critical and doctors placed no prohibition against her being questioned by police.

That task fell to Detective Ronald Marsenison who obtained an account from the young woman about the events of the evening—Donna's date with her beau, the girls' get-together, and their drive to Donna's apartment house where Jody was to drop off her friend and then go to her own home at nearby 1918 Hutchinson River Parkway.

Then Jody went into the significant details about those moments that led up to the shooting: "Donna came back to the car to say something she had forgotten to tell me before. It had something to do with our vacation plans that we were making for this Summer.

"Then all of a sudden a man...he wasn't very tall...appeared on the sidewalk and came toward the car on the side where Donna was sitting. Without saying a word...he pointed a gun with a long barrel and fired two or three shots.

"I believe the first shot hit Donna in the head...She slumped back on the seat. I'm not sure when I was hit...with the second or third shot. But, as you can see, he got me in the thigh..."

What did the killer look like, Marsenison wanted to know?

He had a wide face with a nose whose tip seemed slightly pinched, eyes that "appear to stare at you," and hair that was brown and curly.

"How tall was he...how much would you say he weighed?" the detective asked.

"About 5 feet 8...and I would say he was around 175 pounds," responded the only eyewitness to the murder.

"Would you recognize him if you ever saw him again?" the detective asked.

Jody shook her head with a vigorous up and

down motion.

"I'll never forget him," she said.

Other detectives interrogated Mr. and Mrs. Lauria as well as Donna's brothers, Michael and Louis.

Anyone who might have any reason—no matter how remote, how far-fetched, how unlikely—to harm Donna, they inquired?

There was instant and unanimous agreement that Donna had no enemies.

What did the parents know about Donna's boyfriend, Detectives John Sheridan and Richard Paul pumped?

Why...why ask about him, the parents demanded in disbelief? And in anger, too.

Police investigations often hit on what many consider to be cruel and inhumane approaches in the search for clues and evidence that can conceivably help to solve a crime. No detective was suggesting that the young man Donna planned to marry was even remotely suspected of complicity in the crime. Yet asking questions about him and all others who knew and associated with Donna was part of the routine.

Checking out such innocent, uninvolved persons eliminates them from suspicion and clears the path which authorities must travel on the way to the ultimate solution of that senseless outrage perpetrated in this quiet Bronx neighborhood.

Up in the apartment the detectives were shown mementos of the Lauria's only daughter in hopes that there might be something of help there—a tiny morsel, perhaps—which might yield a clue or lead to the killer.

But it certainly didn't surface in their examination of a clutch of white envelopes containing a Kodachrome vignette of the vivacious dark-haired Donna, whose brown eyes sparkled in every photo—from the innocuous pose seated in an armchair and glancing askance at nothing in particular, like a daydreamer, to the one of her in a stance strongly suggesting a cover girl in the attire of what the well-dressed June bride should wear.

But the white dress Donna had on in that picture wasn't the one she'd planned to wear later in the year when she was to have married her sweetheart. The one for that occasion hadn't been chosen yet—and Donna had wanted Jody Valente to come along and help her make up her mind—just as Mrs. Lauria was to have accompanied her daughter as well to the dressmaker's on that joyful mission.

Donna and Stan had so many plans. One of them was recounted through Mrs. Lauria's trembling lips.

"They were going to buy a house—probably upstate," she related. "They didn't want to live in the city."

"Why?" one of the detectives asked perfunctorily.

"Does that need an answer?" Michael asked tartly. "Look what happened..."

Her parents and brothers then escorted Detectives Sheridan and Paul to Donna's bedroom in the five-room apartment and exhibited some of her favorite possessions.

The room seemed to be overflowing with stuffed toy animals. But there was a real one, too—Donna's pet toy poodle named Beau who was wandering around the room almost aimlessly, now and then scampering through the legs of the visitors, sniffing curiously at their shoes and trousers and perhaps, too, wondering where his mistress might be—but certainly being incapable of knowing that she would never again return.

Michael opened the closet door and let the detectives view his sister's clothes. The rack seemed to grunt under the weight of all the many stylish, mod garments that hung there.

"She wasn't a glamour freak, but she enjoyed dressing up," Michael explained, his voice choked as he recalled the fun he and Lou had had in times past at their only sister's expense.

"We teased her a great deal," Mike went on. "She was a living doll. We used to fight a lot, like most brothers and sisters, I guess. But that wasn't true lately. Lately we'd become great friends. Real great friends, I swear."

Lou nodded in agreement.

"Yes, we had gotten to be very, very close," he said in a voice on the edge of cracking.

Mr. and Mrs. Lauria both wept as their sons described their happy experiences with Donna.

After daybreak, detectives went on a door-to-door search for possible eyewitnesses or for information which could aid the investigation.

No one could add anything more to what the sleuths had already learned. But the neighbors were unanimous in their praises of Donna, who had lived all her life in Pelham Bay Park.

"A lovely girl...very nice, very polite...The whole thing is so senseless...Why Donna...Why...?"

Detectives wished they could explain why a killer stalked out of the night's black shadows and took Donna Lauria's life. Because if they could explain that, then they'd know who the killer was—and they'd have him in custody.

Their investigation at the scene was augmented by the detectives from the Crime Scene Unit. They photographed the street between its two nearest intersections, Mayflower and Pilgrim Avenues; shot numerous interior and exterior photos of the Olds Cutlass (and the corpse as well before it was removed to the morgue for autopsy); dusted the car for fingerprints inside and out; finetoothcombed the street, its gutters, and sidewalks for any conceivable clue—a matchbook cover, a discarded pack of cigarettes, anything that looked as though the killer had dropped or tossed it away—which could help put police on his trail.

The most telling bit of evidence that the teams of detectives ultimately drew out of their investigation was the conclusion of the ballistics experts on the type of weapon used

35

in the crime.

It was a most unusual gun and the two lead slugs found inside the car—one fired wildly and one that had torn through Jody Valente's thigh, along with the one later removed by the medical examiner from the victim's head—gave conclusive proof that the survivor of the savage attack wasn't hallucinating when she reported the assassin had wielded a long-barreled revolver.

Indeed he had, for the three bullets were enormous .44-caliber slugs!

The killer had come armed with a gun right out of the sagebrush and cactus country of the Wild West. It was the same gun that Buffalo Bill and Jessie James and the Dalton Brothers and even Bat Masterson once unlimbered from their holsters when they had reasons to shoot from the hip.

But the man who pulled the trigger of the .44-caliber revolver in the Bronx that early morning of July 29th didn't have the style of the good and badmen of the West when they fired their guns—with one hand.

As Jody Valente explained it vividly and with total certainty to Detectives Marsenison and Paul, this killer held the gun with two hands—one on the grip, the other underneath to steady the trigger finger. He also went into a semi-crouch—the same combat stance that the TV cops affect when aiming or firing their guns at the bad guys.

The unusual caliber of the weapon and the killer's peculiar stance and style of firing the weapon didn't make an immediate impact on the investigators. But in time, this information and evidence would become increasingly more significant and, indeed, indispensable to the case as the search for the psychopathic killer commanded greater numbers and more intense concentration by the posse of lawmen.

Actually it would grow to be an all-important link between the fugitive gunman and the largest police force in the United States that was engaged in the search for him.

But in the hours after Miss Lauria was slain and Miss Valente was wounded, the unexplained attack took its place as a more or less routine crime on an unusually busy midweek night of criminal activity. The killing of Donna Lauria and the wounding of Jody Valente was but one of five separate shooting incidents that confronted detectives in three boroughs and left the statisticians at Police Headquarters shaking their heads in puzzlement at the freakish outbreak of gunfire.

"This is about normal for a Summer weekend but it certainly beats everything for a weekday," offered Deputy Police Commissioner Frank McLoughlin, the department's liaison with the press. He was making that observation in the cold light of dawn after the series of violent crimes had ended.

The shootings had begun at 7:30 o'clock the previous evening on Ninth Street, between Avenues C and D, on the Lower East Side, hard by the towering filigree steeled Williamsburgh Bridge.

An unidentified sniper felled a man walking along the crowded street.

Forty minutes later, another man was shot and wounded by a gunman in hiding, this time on Eighth Street, again between Avenues C and D.

At 10 p.m., still another pedestrian was gunned down by a triggerman firing from concealed quarters. Incredibly, this shooting happened on Sixth Street—again between the same Avenues C and D.

Police of the Ninth Precinct viewed the three shootings as "random, unrelated, and perpetrated by three different gunmen."

If it were fiction, who'd have believed that three men could be wounded in separate attacks by different assailants within two-and-a-half hours and a mere three short blocks of each other?

Over that Williamsburgh Bridge in Brooklyn, shortly before midnight, nineteen-year-old Dennis Adams and twenty-two-year-old Neil Lewis, both from Manhattan's East 28th Street, were accosted in front of 3303 Foster Avenue in Brooklyn's Flatbush section by a hostile youth.

Adams and Lewis tried to avoid the encounter but the stranger, in his teens and obviously searching for trouble, pulled a gun from his pocket, shot both men, and fled. The victims were taken by ambulance to Kings County Hospital, with Adams in critical condition.

At almost the very second that Donna

Lauria and Jody Valente were being set upon by the killer brandishing the .44-caliber revolver, Police Officer Steven Trimingham, some eighteen miles to the south and doing the midnight to 8 a.m. tour at the East 67th Street stationhouse, spotted three suspicious men and decided to follow them.

It was exactly 1 a.m. when he began the tail along Madison Avenue near 64th Street. What had aroused his misgivings about the trio was their furtive manner and, even of more dubious appearance, the paper bag one of them was carrying in hand.

Just as they approached the corner of Madison and 64th, the three men had become aware of the blue uniform stalking them. They slowed their gait and muttered among themselves.

Then the man carrying the paper bag wheeled and pulled a sawed-off shotgun out of the sack. He raised it to his shoulder and pulled the trigger.

Trimingham was a mere step ahead of the would-be assassin. Suspecting the man was capable of pulling such a stunt, the cop dove into the street between two parked cars just as the blast burst in a roar of fire from the muzzle and showered the sidewalk with the deadly pellets.

Now with his .38-caliber revolver in hand and cocked just in case, Trimingham leaped out of his shelter and seized twenty-seven-year-old Raoul Diaz who had no intention of resisting arrest for attempted murder.

But Diaz's companions didn't wait around after the shotgun roared with its lethal discharge. They fled around the corner into East 64th Street and disappeared into the wind.

By now, up in the Bronx, Donna Lauria was dead and Jody Valente was in the hospital. For the next four hours, there weren't any shootings in the city.

However, at 5:15 a.m. at another Bronx locale some six miles from the borough's "peaceful" Baychester-Pelham Bay area, the last of the dreadful night's epidemic of motiveless shootings occurred.

It was on a street corner not far from Raoul Diaz's South Bronx neighborhood of East 138th Street—where rows upon rows of tenements and once-proud apartment buildings lie in ruins, burned-out shells and hulks as a result of the fires set in them by the savages we spoke of earlier who roam the Bronx like barbarians laying waste whatever structures of civilization loom in front of them.

Three men now, Moses Baldwin, 26, Tom Branch, 37, and Clarence Gray, 52, all from the neighborhood, were saying goodnight to each other after a tour of the town.

Suddenly three men approached. Although all were strangers to the group in conversation, the rifle in the hands of one of the intruders was not. Without provocation the rifleman opened fire at the feet of the three men. He pumped bullets from his automatic

.22-caliber Winchester at will—like in Westerns to make the other guy dance a jig.

Baldwin, Branch, and Gray screamed out in pain as each in turn was hit in his lower legs by the fusillade.

Then just as quickly as the assailant and his companions appeared, they were out of sight, jumping into a waiting car which had a fourth man behind the wheel, and roared away.

The three victims were taken to Bronx Lebanon Hospital where they were treated for relatively minor bullet wounds and released.

That was the end of the night of terror when rampaging gunmen visited an unsuspecting city and left one dead, nine wounded, and an eleventh intended victim a lucky near-miss.

It was now a little after 9 o'clock on that Thursday morning of July 29th and the pilgrimmage of relatives and friends and neighbors had begun to the fourth floor of the Buhre Avenue Apartments where Mr. and Mrs. Lauria and their two sons sat inconsolably around the dining room table.

One by one, grief-stricken visitors shuffled through the door and conveyed their condolences to Donna Lauria's parents and brothers.

Now and then a caller embraced Rose and murmured consoling words in her ear.

"Look at her," Mrs. Lauria would say at times, holding up one of the photos that earlier had been shown to the detectives. They were the pictures of Donna in the flowing white dress that could have been a pose for *Vogue* or *Bride* or any of the other slicks; and the pictures of Donna sitting relaxed in the armchair, and the many others.

"She's gone...she's gone...my little baby girl..." Mrs. Lauria wept.

Other mourners put their hands in a gentle touch on Michael's shoulder and he looked up through red-rimmed eyes to acknowledge the gesture which meant more than words at a time when he was so bereft over the loss of his only daughter.

The brothers also took cognizance of the sympathetic words and other forms of silent expression many visitors conveyed when they couldn't express their grief and sorrow orally.

As senseless and as motiveless as the killing of Donna Lauria and the wounding of Jody Valente might have seemed, no instant fear was generated to suggest even remotely that it was of a contagious, city-wide dimension then.

Even the police investigating the case couldn't get too aroused over the episode, even though it had burnished its traumatic and tragic imprint on the Lauria family and spread a very real, yet only temporary fear in their quiet Bronx neighborhood where such crimes are never likely to be forgotten but are also not very likely to strike a permanent terror among the residents—so long as it doesn't happen again.

Little did the people of that North Bronx

community see what was coming as they remained smug in their feeling of safety and seeming immunity from the pestilence of murders, assaults, robberies, burglaries, rapes, and other violences afflicting so many other sections of the city.

It would be some months more before those people would all at once come to sense trepidation and react in near-panic at the true meaning of violence as it finally came to haunt the folks of that "safe" Baychester-Pelham Bay region.

No one—not even the police who investigated Donna Lauria's baffling murder—could envision then what time would bring:

The deep, abiding, vivid fear of a psychopathic assassin with an inexplicable, unquenchable penchant to kill and maim girls with long, brown hair.

The .44-caliber killer...

CHAPTER III

AFTER A FRIDAY NIGHT
ROCK MOVIE...

November 26 was a Friday night and the bone-chilling snap of another approaching Winter was in the air everywhere. Certainly it was too late in the season to have hoped for continued warm weather.

Thanksgiving was a day gone already and a mere twenty-four shopping days remained to Christmas—unless one numbered the four extra gift-searching days in shops doing business on Sundays now that New York's ancient blue laws had gone into discard.

Friday night in the Floral Park section of Queens was never much different than in so many other areas of the city where teenagers congregate. They gather on a favorite street-corner, in a special hamburger hangout, or even at an out-of-the-way neighborhood discotheque where they might quaff a beer or two with a phony or forged I. D. card that adds a critical few months to meet the minimum age standards of the Alcoholic Beverage Commission for drinking.

But on that Friday night, eighteen-year-old Joanne Lomino and sixteen-year-old Donna DeMasi had followed a more circuitous route to their preferred hamburger stand. They had first journeyed by bus and subway to Times

44

Square and the Broadway scene for an evening at a rock movie.

The show let out shortly after 10:30 p.m. and Joanne and Donna were feeling some hunger by now. They could go for a thick, juicy hamburger with all the trimmings and a milk shake—but certainly not on the Gay White Way. Not the way it was those days, a deteriorated, seemingly endless tapestry of pornography and prostitution, with undesirables lurking at every corner and darkened doorway to solicit or dispense the illicit favors merchandised by the dregs of society.

Joanne and Donna fitted their half-dollar tokens into the turnstile slots and rode the graffiti-covered subway to the IND line's Hillside Avenue station, the last stop. Then they caught the bus which ran further on along Hillside Avenue, from Hollis to the city line for another 50-cent fare.

They got off at the corner of 257th Street in Floral Park, which was the site of a late-hours hamburger stand the kids of the neighborhood really dug.

After a satisfying snack and an exchange of pleasantries with some of the crowd—many of them neighborhood youngsters who attended nearby Martin Van Buren High School in Queens Village—Joanne and Donna left the corner burger shop and walked homeward in the quiet, virtually crime-free middle-class neighborhood of neat, detached one-family homes which abut the Nassau County line and a sister community, also called Floral Park.

Joanne Lomino lived at 83-31 261st Street, which lies between 83rd and Hillside Avenues. Donna DeMasi's home was four blocks further on, at 86-29 262nd Street, situated between 86th and 87th Avenues.

Since Joanne's home was more or less on the way to where Donna lived, the latter walked her friend to her house and sat with her on the front stoop to talk a while.

The time was 12:30 a.m.

It was slightly overcast and the chill of approaching Winter was very definitely in the Autumn air, although it was still pleasant to be outdoors.

While they had enjoyed their night out at the rock movie and their repast at the hamburger haven, Joanne and Donna weren't altogether in the happiest frames of mind nor were they living through the best of times

Their spirits had been dampened by divergent discouragements.

A former student at Van Buren High, Joanne was in the dumps because she'd just been laid off from work; Donna, a sophomore at Van Buren, was feeling blue because she'd just had a spat and a split with her boyfriend.

And it was those separate problems besetting the two pretty teenagers with long, flowing brown hair that reached down to their shoulders which had occupied their thoughts and conversation in front of Joanne's pleasant two-story, white-shingled house. The enclosed porch and the black wrought iron rail protectively flanked the three-step concrete stoop where the girls had sat to chat.

After ten minutes or so had passed, Joanne and Donna decided to call it a night.

Joanne rose to her feet and descended the steps to the sidewalk. Donna got up and reached into her purse for the key to unlock the front door.

"Goodnight," she said in a whisper, not wanting to disturb the neighborhood. "See you tomorrow..."

Before Joanne could respond, there was an interruption caused by the sighting of an unfamiliar figure walking on the opposite sidewalk of 83rd Avenue.

The girls might not have given the stranger a second thought had it not been for the startling turn in direction he took after spotting them in front of Joanne's house. As he abruptly changed course he also quickened his pace appreciably.

After crossing at the corner of 261st Street to the other side of the avenue, he headed straight toward Joanne and Donna, who stood their ground, more in puzzlement than fright.

Yet concern was not completely absent from their thoughts as the man came into sight more clearly after passing under the street light.

He looked to be about thirty years old, perhaps 5 feet 10, or a little shorter, and about 150 pounds or a slight bit heavier. He was wearing an Army-type pea green, three-quarter length coat for warmth against the early morning cold, now being lofted over the area by a rising wind sweeping in from nearby Little Neck Bay, a large, friendly inlet of Long Island Sound which provides a safe, sheltered haven for thousands of sailing craft and motor cruisers for the area's ever-growing number of seasonal sailors.

Still, neither girl felt any particular deep apprehension as the man moved closer, closer, ever closer. To Joanne and Donna it seemed he might be lost, that he was coming to them to seek directions.

And for a brief, fleeting moment their assumption appeared a correct one as the stranger blurted, "Say, can you tell me how to get to..."

Then, all at once, his words became inaudible and just as quickly faded away. An instant later, Joanne Lomino and Donna DeMasi shrieked in abject horror.

The man had yanked a gun from his waistband and without a word began firing at the girls.

Donna cried in anguish as a slug tore through the fleshy part of her neck and shattered her collarbone. The impact came with such force that she was toppled backward to the sidewalk, a fall later credited with probably having saved Donna from more serious injury or even death had she remained on her feet and been struck by another of the four bullets the gunman had fired.

48

But not all of the three other lead slugs went astray. One of them plowed into Joanne Lomino's back just as she had turned and was trying to unlock the door to summon her family's help.

Joanne collapsed on the concrete stoop with a pitiful, agonizing scream.

By now lights in the Lomino house and others in the block were flicked on as Joanne's family and neighbors heard the girls' startling screams of pain.

Ben Taormina, who lived next door, pulled on his pants without even looking out the window. He was out of the house in something like a minute. As he would soon tell Detective Bernard Judge of the 105th Squad in Queens Village:

"I saw Donna lying on the stoop, screaming that she was dying. Her jacket was soaked through with blood. She was in terrible shape.

"I saw Joanne just sort of leaning against the door of the house, not saying anything much. She didn't seem to be hurt that badly because she wasn't bleeding that much."

Taormina said he didn't see the assailant.

But another neighbor did catch a glimpse of the fugitive.

"I just got a fleeting look," the detective was told by the eyewitness whose identity was not revealed by authorities because this person would be called upon to identify the gunman—if and when he was caught.

"What can you tell me about him?" Judge asked the witness.

The man's height, weight, and clothing, which the witness described, dovetailed precisely with the portrait of the assassin that Donna had painted for police interrogators. They had questioned her in the emergency room of Long Island Jewish-Hillside Medical Center in nearby New Hyde Park, before she was wheeled to surgery for repairs to her shattered collarbone.

Detectives were unable to speak to Joanne Lomino because her condition was critical. The bullet which struck her back had lodged in her spine. Her legs were paralyzed and, as she was taken to surgery, doctors gave her small chance of regaining the use of her lower extremities.

Back where the crime was committed, the Crime Scene Unit and specialists from the police laboratory went through the rigorous routine of gathering whatever shreds of evidence the mysterious gunman might have left behind.

But there were scant few clues to recover. Aside from the bullet that doctors removed from Donna's collarbone and the other one from Joanne's spine—both so badly shattered and crushed that riflings couldn't be determined—the ballistics sleuths also gathered up the other two slugs that the gunman had fired.

The latter pair were in far better condition than the bullets that had lodged in the girls' bodies. One of the strays had struck the metal mailbox, the other was imbedded in the wooden front door.

These bullets would be analyzed later by ballistics experts and the barrel markings were to tell a revealing tale: that those slugs were fired from the very same .44-caliber *Wild West* type revolver that had killed Donna Lauria and wounded Jody Valenti four months earlier in the Northeast Bronx.

But did that finding strike an immediate recognition for the investigators of the Queens shooting?

Did the discovery prompt detectives in the Bronx to leap into action and make tracks to Queens to compare notes with the sleuths probing Joanne Lomino's and Donna DeMasi's shootings?

No, the ballistics findings didn't precipitate such action even though it was a mere ten miles from the Baychester-Pelham Bay neighborhood where Miss Lauria died and her friend Jody Valente was wounded to the Floral Park neighborhood across the merging waters of the East River and Pelham Bay in Queens.

In fact, there were several direct express highway links between the two neighborhoods in the separate boroughs—roads that no one, not even a psychopathic gunman, would encounter difficulty traversing from one locale to the other in fifteen minutes or so.

Of course the man who murdered and maimed in the Bronx may not have traveled between those two points on the same night that he wounded the two Queens teenagers.

Conceivably he could have been a Queens resident and not a Bronxite. Yet neither of these theoretical possibilities was explored by the cops, nor any others—because nobody, but nobody, in the NYPD had as yet tied the two attacks to the same assassin or even the same gun, although that evidence was, as the cliché goes, in the palms of their hands.

True, the crimes had been committed four months apart. But is the time factor an excuse for the abdication of responsibility in criminal investigations—responsibility to check out every possible angle and seek to find a possible link or similarity with other cases?

Had the police recognized that there was a startling connection between the two crimes and alerted each other to that situation—to the possibility the gunman may reside either in the Baychester-Pelham Bay area of the Bronx, scene of his first strike, or in the Floral Park-Glen Oaks section of Queens, site of his second attack—then stakeouts by a task force of detectives under a single, unified command over both areas might conceivably have prevented the terrible grief and tragic consequences yet to come.

By not being alert to the unmistakable evidence that the Bronx and Queens crimes were committed by the same deranged assassin, the man who would ultimately become known as the .44-caliber killer, the police had given him precious time to preserve his anonymity and suppress the notoriety that was yet to be attached to his frightful and murderous rampages.

In their investigation in Queens, detectives of the 105th Squad made no inroads in picking up the gunman's trail. The one solid witness, the one whose identity was kept under wraps, had also seen the assassin in flight, was the best link with the fugitive.

"He ran quickly at first, the gun with its barrel held in his left hand as he went," the witness told authorities. "Then when he reached the corner, I saw him slow down and begin walking. And that's when he disappeared from my view, when he turned the corner. Then he was gone..."

Did the witness hear a car start, or a car driven away?

"No, nothing at all," the witness responded. "Just the two girls crying and whimpering...that's all that broke the silence of the night, that's all I heard...except for the shots that woke me and brought me to my window..."

Within a week, Donna DeMasi had recovered sufficienty to warrant her discharge from the hospital. She went home to convalesce, just as her older brothers, Michael and Daniel, announced the posting of a $1000 cash reward for information leading to the solution of the shooting.

"We'll pay on the barrelhead as soon as the guy who shot our sister and Joanne Lomino is arrested, prosecuted, and convicted," vowed Michael.

Meanwhile, police went through two additional routines as part of the investigation—as they would have done in any investigation.

The first was in establishing a special phone—740-0600—that was to be called by anyone with information about the case.

The second was in having a police artist draw a sketch of the assailant after sitting with Donna DeMasi at her home and having her describe his features. The artist also visited Joanne Lomino's bedside at Long Island Jewish-Hillcrest for her recollections about the gunman's looks and appearance, to further help in the preparation of the composite sketch.

Their description, coupled with what the unidentified neighbor had contributed to the artist, resulted in a sketch of a man with a wide face and a nose whose tip seemed slightly pinched, eyes that had a cold, steely look, and brown curly hair.

Wasn't that the same description that Jody Valente had provided another police artist four months earlier when she was interviewed for the sketch prepared in the search for the .44-caliber gunman who'd wounded Jody and killed her friend Donna Lauria?

Yes, almost identical in every detail.

But did the sketch of the Bronx assassin and the one now prepared in Queens strike a recognition in the 28,000-member police department at that time in early December when both wanted posters were tacked on bulletin boards in every precinct in the city?

Did anyone say, "Hey, the guy who did the
54

number on those girls in the Bronx looks like the one who plugged those two kids in Queens?"

No, no one said that.

The concentration of the searches remained in separate commands, divided and isolated by the waters of the East River which merge with those of Pelham Bay, then mix with Little Neck Bay and flow into the dominant body of water known as Long Island Sound.

It was the same police department, yet the Bronx had apparently no idea what was going on in Queens. And Queens had no clue as to what was happening in the Bronx.

In fact, the detectives and uniformed officers of the Nassau County Police Department's Floral Park Precinct had more of a hand in the Queens investigation, which wasn't even their legal jurisdiction.

They had been asked to help in the search for the gunman in the early morning hours on the chance that after he had shot Joanne Lomino and Donna DeMasi, he fled into Nassau. Their search, of course, turned up no trace of the .44-caliber assassin.

There were other similar parallels in the Floral Park shooting and the one on the early morning of July 29th when Miss Lauria was killed and Miss Valente was wounded.

Remember all those other shootings around town that Summer night which tended to confuse and confound the situation in the Bronx?

Well, in Queens the situation was no

different in November. There'd been two other shootings in the southeastern part of the borough. These contributed a distraction and possible diversion from Floral Park of an immediate higher concentration and priority of manpower that is always most vital in the first hours after a crime, when the clues are freshest and the fugitive's trail is hottest.

Nine hours before Joanne Lomino and Donna DeMasi were gunned down, a 29-year-old apartment dweller in Rochdale Village, was shot in the back and wounded critically.

Mrs. Marion Gibbs had just dumped garbage into the building's incinerator and was returning to her apartment on the sixth floor when two men suddenly bolted out of a staircase landing.

One drew a gun. Mrs. Gibbs screamed and dashed for the safety of her apartment. But the man opened fire and the bullet plowed into her back.

Mrs. Gibbs was rushed to the hospital in critical condition. Detectives who investigated the case said they couldn't come up with a motive.

A similar, seemingly motiveless shooting occurred several hours after Miss Lomino and Miss DeMasi were wounded. Thomas Nelson, 16, was shot at 6:15 a.m. as he was walking on 115th Drive, near 115th Street in the high-crime area of Jamaica.

Nelson, who was taken to Mary Immaculate Hospital with a flesh wound, told police that a car with three men had stopped at the intersection and one of the passengers in the back seat pegged several shots at him.

One of the bullets clipped Nelson in the lower leg.

Of course the assailants who wounded Nelson and shot Mrs. Gibbs were different gunmen, and neither one was the assassin who fired the long-barreled, deadly .44-caliber revolver in Floral Park.

After the initial early high level of investigatory activity given to most serious crimes had run the gamut without substantial results, the case was slowly relegated to the back burner as other more violent crimes commanded the attention directed earlier in full force to Donna's and Joanne's assault.

As one detective put it:

"It's a very strange case. We can't find a motive or a clue. As far as we know, the girls didn't provoke or argue with the man who shot them. All I can say, this is not something that usually occurs out here. It may never happen again..."

CHAPTER IV

DEATH BEFORE
ST. VALENTINE'S DAY

He was behind the wheel of his sedan and she was seated beside him in the front seat just after returning from a glorious Saturday night date. Because they were planning to marry in the near future, the couple seldom saw each other during the week. They were both hard at work building up their nest egg that would enable them to enjoy financial independence and to cope rather than struggle as so many young marrieds are inclined to do.

So, only the weekends were their own.

And now, this Saturday night out together was rapidly coming to a close, although there was still a little left to do on their itinerary. Neither 30-year-old John Diel nor his 26-year-old sweetheart were anxious to say their goodnights just yet. It was 12:30 a.m., merely half past midnight of that frigid morning of January 30, 1977, a Sunday.

Besides the dance they were going to, Christine and John wanted to talk about their engagement party which was just two weeks away—on St. Valentine's Day. This would be followed a few months afterward, in the early Summer, with the dream of marriage

58

fulfilled after a long seven years in the making.

To all who knew them, Christine Freund and John Diel were a delightful and compatible couple; they were also regarded as being industrious, persevering, and level-headed.

Perhaps it was their backgrounds that made them that way. Both had emigrated with their parents from neighboring European countries. Their separate trans-Atlantic trails ultimately led both families to the borough of Queens.

The Freunds came to America in 1957 from Austria, the Diels from Yugoslavia.

Christine and her family settled into a comfortable home at 59-18 Linden Street in the Ridgewood section. That was almost a month or thereabouts before Diel and his parents made their move from the Old Country and came to live in a pleasant home at 61-58 Gates Avenue in the same Ridgewood community.

Living there as neighbors, it was not surprising that the attractive, shapely Christine and the handsome, vigorously athletic John should meet. It was at a Saturday night dance in 1970. If there is any truth to the old saw about love at first sight, it applied unequivocally to this couple.

They were hooked on each other from the start. Through the years, they always planned marriage but the time was never right because they both wanted "to do it right," as John often told his family and friends. But time brought them closer to their mutual goal, although their work kept them apart most of the time.

Christine's days were devoted to her job as a secretary for Reynolds Securities. She worked in their Midtown Manhattan offices on 42nd Street.

Yet while his own days were free, John's nights were not because he worked as bartender at the Ridgewood-3 Restaurant.

So except for a brief time the last Summer at a mountain retreat where they'd vacationed together, their only opportunity to be with each other was weekends which took in Saturday night dates for movies and dancing and snacking, Sunday afternoons, now and then, watching soccer games.

Or, for Diel occasionally, playing with the amateur groups of German, Austrian, Italian, Greek, and English teams that kept the sport alive on New York City's sandlots before the Cosmos brought soccer into its own and set a North American crowd record of 77,000 at the Giants Stadium in New Jersey's Meadowlands Sports Complex.

On that Saturday night of January 29th, John and Christine had laid out their itinerary in advance and followed it precisely as planned. They began their evening by going to the Continental Theater at 70-20 Austin Street in Forest Hills, not too far from their Ridgewood neighborhood.

The movie was *Rocky*, a love story with a

plot not too unlike their own tender-sweet romance.

After the theater they walked to the nearby Wine Gallery where Christine and John had a late evening treat of cheese and crackers and wine. Now with midnight past, the young lovers' schedule called for one more stop on their excursion before calling it a night—the Masonic dance in Ridgewood Hall, the very center of their first meeting seven years ago.

They had not planned to stay too long at the dance because Christine had much to do the next day—the planning and preparations with her mother, Olga, and other members of the family for the Valentine's Day engagement party at the Freund house.

But later in the day, after dinner, Christine would drop into John's house as she did almost every Sunday, a time for a family gathering at the Diels' modest but comfortable and ample home. John's brother and sister-in-law and their young children would be there along with the parents—as would be John and Chris, occupying a cozy corner of the couch, watching TV or just talking.

It was just about 12:30 a.m. when they left the Wine Gallery. Christine snuggled close to her beau, her long-flowing brown tresses brushing against John's full mod beard. They felt warmth that way in the teeth-shattering cold as they walked arm in arm on Forest Hills' quiet, crime-free streets toward their car, parked in Station Square, opposite the

61

Forest Hills Inn and the Long Island Rail Road station.

As they reached their destination, John and Christine unclinched from their embrace and she walked to the door on the passenger side of the car, alongside the curb. He went to the driver's side and unlocked the door. He checked his watch in the light cast by a mercury vapor lamp on the opposite side of the square and said something to Christine over the roof of the car about there being still lots of time to make it to the dance.

Once seated behind the wheel, Diel reached over and unlatched the door so Christine could get in.

Meanwhile, he started the engine. It coughed and sputtered from the cold, but soon it was racing.

"Better warm it up a bit," he murmured, putting his arm around Christine and pulling her close to him.

She returned his embrace and they clinched in a kiss for several long seconds. Finally John and Christine settled back in their seats for the short ride to Ridgewood Hall.

Diel was about to shift into gear when an ear-splitting roar and a terrifying crash of glass made him rear back in fright. The first explosion was followed instantaneously by a second. Then a deafening silence settled over the scene.

For a moment his mind was a blank. An instant later he was fully alerted to the reality of what had just happened. He realized it after he felt Christine's head sag onto his right shoulder.

"Chris!" he cried out. "What's wrong? Chris, are you all right?"

There was no response.

He reached out and touched his sweet-heart's face. Suddenly his stomach knurled and he began perspiring profusely. That reaction was generated by the warm wetness he felt on Christine's face.

It was blood!

Though seized totally by this horrific and unexpected turn, Diel held staunchly to courage, not panic. He sensed that Christine had been shot. How badly he couldn't know. Yet the blood, flowing from a point over her right ear and her seemingly comotose state told him that the condition was serious, if not critical—or even fatal.

With his left hand he pulled the latch and threw the door open. Then taking hold of Christine by the shoulders, he eased her down as gently as he could so that her head rested on the warm seat he had just moved from.

Then, slamming the door shut, he ran along the darkened, deserted street in search of someone, anyone, who might summon an ambulance or a doctor or any sort of help.

"Help! Help! I need help!" he yelled as he ran, aimlessly, almost blindly in a direction he chose only because it was a way to go. But it proved to have been the right one, for when he reached the corner of Burns Street and 71st Avenue his cries, now at a hysterical level, were heard by a young couple passing in a car.

They stopped. He told them what had happened. They asked him to hop in. They drove back to his car so he could stay with Christine while they sped off to get the police.

Within minutes, the familiar blue and white police cruisers, their dome lights ablaze, sirens screaming, roared one after another to a stop beside Diel's car.

"Can't depend on an ambulance," one of the uniformed police officers wisely decided. "Let's take her in the car."

The policemen lifted Christine out of the front seat and carried her to one of the cruisers. They laid her down on the back seat and her beau, squeezing in the floor area on his knees to comfort her, shouted, "We're ready...please go to the hospital right now."

The police car raced at near 80 mph speeds to St. John's Hospital in nearby Elmhurst and pulled to a screeching stop at the emergency entrance.

A rolling stretcher was wheeled out and Christine was brought inside. Doctors, alerted ahead of time by police to expect a victim with a head wound, were standing by to receive the patient. A neurosurgeon had also been summoned after the hospital learned that the victim had suffered a critical head wound.

Besides the bleeding from over the right ear, Christine had also suffered a wound of lesser severity on the right shoulder. The doctors agreed that both punctures had been caused by bullets—large caliber bullets!

And as police would soon learn, after ballistics examined the slugs taken from the victim and a third one that ricocheted off the windshield, they were the same deadly .44-caliber bullets that earlier had felled four victims, one fatally. Preparations were quickly made to perform surgery on Christine in the hope of removing the bullet which, as X-rays showed, had lodged in her brain. It was, of course, one of the most precarious operations any surgeon could perform. For the plate, or negatives, showed that the bullet was lodged in a portion of the brain that condemned Christine to a life of total paralysis—even if the neurosurgeon could have extracted the bullet without destroying too much tissue.

As it turned out, Christine Freund succumbed at 4:30 a.m. that Sunday before she could be taken to the operating room.

Now, finally and at last, the police began to sense the outside possibility that Miss Freund's death could conceivably have had some link or relationship with the other seemingly senseless shootings of recent months—those of Donna Lauria and Jody Valente and of Joanne Lomino and Donna DeMasi.

And, oh, yes, that of a factory worker named Carl Denaro, who was shot on a street in Flushing, Queens, the previous October.

Some of the momentum for discovery was undoubtedly generated by enterprising newsmen from the city's three dailies who were putting together stories that the senseless slaying of Christine Freund was conceivably the work of the same man who shot the Floral Park girls and killed and wounded the two young women in the Bronx.

The stories soon spurred attention—and action—by Mayor Abraham D. Beame and Police Commissioner Michael J. Codd. They ordered greatly intensified investigations.

Sergeant Richard Conlon, of the 15th Homicide Zone in Queens, questioned Diel, who described his night out with his sweetheart and their return to the car.

"While the engine was warming up," Diel told Conlon, "Chris and I kissed. We were in the car at most two minutes and we were just ready to take off when all of a sudden I heard a crash. The window came in. It didn't sound like a firecracker, it was a very much louder bang. Chris slumped over onto my shoulder... Then, when I felt the blood and realized she was in great trouble, I left her there and ran to call the police."

After his interview with Diel, Conlon was confronted by newsmen for an explanation of the shooting.

"We're searching criminal and mental hospital records for a possible lead," he said. "We're going for the time being on the theory that the gunman is probably the same one who committed three similar crimes in the past seven months."

He was referring now to the Lauria-Valente case in the Bronx, the Lomino-DeMasi case in Queens—and the wounding of Carl Denaro.

"I'll admit," continued Conlon, "that evidence tying the four similar shootings together is scarce. But if I had to guess I'd say there's a nut running around.

"The reason we're leaning to the one-man theory is that we've not come up with any suggestion of what motive is behind the shootings. So far as the people involved are concerned, they're absolutely clean."

Conlon disclosed that there'd been a strong public response to the police department's call for information.

Mental hospital records on recently-discharged inmates were checked and even police files were gone over for any suggestion of a pattern which might show a similar modus operandi with any of the four shootings.

But patterns and modus operandis were unnecessary now. Ballistics already knew that each and every bullet tested from each and every one of the four shootings had been fired from the same .44-caliber revolver. The riflings on all the slugs were identical!

No progress in the killing of Christine Freund was made for several days. Then on February 3rd detectives finally uncovered a lead they felt was stronger than anything they had dug up until then.

The sleuths launched a search for two persons, a driver and his passenger who were in a car which had pulled into the Long Island Rail Road station early Sunday morning.

The man who got out of the late-model green

compact with a black top was carrying a large suitcase. It struck at least one eyewitness with the notion that the man was a hitchhiker.

The police investigation determined that an eastbound train had been due in shortly after 1 a.m. and that the stranger very well may have caught that train.

Further information developed by the investigation determined that the man actually asked a commuter for directions to the eastbound platform.

Conlon then explained with great precision why the police wanted to talk to the man:

"We want to know whether he saw something we are desperate to know about—an eyewitness observation of how the killer approached the car, from where he fired, and what escape route he took. If such a person was there at the time, I'm confident he can give us invaluable information because the railroad station affords a good view of the crime area..."

Police appealed to anyone knowing the identities of either the driver of the car or the hitchhiker-passenger to call police at 845-2267 or 520-2900. Of course, the authorities promised all calls would be kept in strictest confidence.

As fifty detectives scoured the borough of Queens for clues, John Diel let a writer in his house and introduced him to his mother. Then together Mrs. Diel and her son brought out an album.

"This is Chris and me up in the mountains,"

Diel said with tears shimmering in his eyes. "But the regular Saturday dates we had together were the real fun thing. We always looked forward to them. Each one came after a week of looking forward to the date. And we always had such beautiful times together..."

He spoke about their impending engagement on St. Valentine's Day and of their marriage that was to have taken place soon after.

"We took a long time getting around to it, but it was something we both wanted to do right. We'd been saving our pay. We had worked like dogs every day of every week throughout the years—except for the short vacations we took.

"And, of course, we always looked forward to our dates on weekends when we were both free..."

Diel's voice plummeted into silence for a brief few seconds as he seemed to search for words to describe what he felt for Christine.

After exhibiting a raft of pictures, Diel spoke about the Sunday nights that Christine spent at the house watching TV while John's brother and the rest of the family were doing their own thing at the Diels' Ridgewood residence.

Diel talked without letup about the girl he was going to marry. Then all at once he looked askance in the room. Tears suddenly filled his eyes.

"This, I'm never going to take off," he said in a choked voice, pulling at a silver chain around his neck.

"This was a gift from Christine," he stammered. "When I came home after it happened, I cried the whole day... I'm sitting here now and I don't know what or why or how... why anybody wanted to kill my beautiful girl..."

Behind him his mother was sobbing now. After several long minutes she raised her arms up high and blurted:

"I can't think it's true... I can't believe it... no way anybody can tell me that Chris is dead... murdered..."

Her words echoed on as her son recalled momentarily the blood he felt when his sweetheart collapsed in his embrace.

"I thought it was a dream for a moment or so... but then I knew it was true. It happened. I was there. It happened. The woman who was going to be my wife died in my arms when some crazy, raving maniac shot a bullet into her head..."

His voice trailed off again. John Diel was spent. He had nothing more to say about the incredibly senseless murder of Christine Freund.

The task of catching her killer was up to the police now. There was no doubt that their work had been cut out for them.

But hold on!

Were the police investigating the murders of two young women, the wounding of three others now?

Or were they really also probing the shooting of a young man who was felled by a bullet while on a date with his girlfriend?

They were!

CHAPTER V

A VICTIM OVERLOOKED

It is of extreme interest to go back to the Autumn night of October 22, 1976.

Twenty-year-old Carl Denaro, who'd been wearing his dark brown hair long—down to his shoulders, in fact—went on a date with a twenty-year-old girlfriend, Rosemary Keenan who, paradoxically, had relatively shorter hair than her beau.

Their date went past the hour when Cinderella's coach turns into a pumpkin, but Rosemary and Carl had no fear her small sports car would suffer that fate. Not even when the clock struck two on that Saturday morning. Denaro and Miss Keenan had an appointment with friends at a neighborhood tavern and they were very near their rendezvous.

At that precise point in time they were in the parking lot of the tavern at 159th Street and 32nd Avenue in Flushing, another Queens community not too far from Forest Hills where Christine Freund was fated to be wounded fatally some three months later.

Rosemary, who'd driven the car to the tavern, had tooled it nose first into one of the stalls and turned off the ignition. She was just reaching the door handle when a frightful series of rapid explosions caused them both to bolt upright in their seats.

As Denaro, a factory worker, was to recall at a much later time, he felt a "ping" in his head and, besides the bang, bang, banging of what he soon sensed was gunfire, he also heard the crashing sound of broken glass.

The "ping" he felt actually was a .44-caliber bullet which tore through the rear window of the car and plowed into his skull. He lapsed into unconsciousness a second or two later, but he remembers now not having any idea that he'd been shot.

Already terrified by the noise, Miss Keenan was aghast at the sight of blood trickling from her boyfriend's head and seeing him pass out. She bolted out of the car and rushed into the tavern screaming for help.

The friends who'd been waiting for the couple ran to the car and sized up the situation. They agreed on the urgency of getting Denaro to the hospital without the delay that waiting for an ambulance would entail.

With one of the friends steadying Denaro in the passenger seat, another jumped behind the wheel and sped to Flushing Hospital and Medical Center.

There Denaro was also found to have suffered a laceration in the middle finger of his right hand, but the head wound was by far the more grave. He was taken to surgery and in an operation that took the better part of two hours, a team of neurosurgeons removed a sliver of lead that appeared to be a severed bullet.

Where the rest of the slug was did not concern the surgeons who had other more pressing needs to attend to. Denaro's skull bone where the bullet struck had splintered. The doctors repaired the damage but had to put a small metal plate in the patient's head to compensate for the bone that had been destroyed.

Denaro, who came within an inch of losing his life—that's how closely the bullet missed his brain—also sustained permanent damage to the middle finger.

"But I thank God I'm still alive to talk about it," Denaro told detectives who interviewed him after he had entered his period of convalescence at the hospital.

Why, everyone on the police investigation wanted to know, would anyone want to shoot Carl Denaro, the young man with the long, shoulder-length brown hair?

He had no enemies that he could think of, knew of no one who'd want to harm him.

"I'm baffled," he told the detectives.

So were the sleuths who worked out of the 109th Squad in the Flushing Precinct. This was a time, remember, when the cops had no idea that a .44-caliber killer had initiated a systematized reign of terror upon the city. There'd been only one attack before Denaro was shot—upon Donna Lauria and Jody Valente in the Bronx.

So what compelling force was there for the cops from Flushing to connect their case with that one when, five weeks later, the detectives from the 105th who handled the more volatile and much more widely-publicized Lomino-DeMasi case didn't have the foggiest notion that theirs had a direct link with the Bronx case—and even to the one next door to them, the Denara shooting?

After all, the boys from the 105th with the gold shields shouldn't be expected to possess any greater powers of observation and deduction or investigative skills than their counterparts at the 109th. The NYPD is a democraticly-run force; every precinct gets an equal share of the superb talent developed at the police academy and the experience acquired from serving in the ranks.

To look at it another way, you could say the cops who investigated the DeMasi-Lomino shooting gave it the well-known "lick-and-a-promise" treatment. In Flushing the effort was more professional as we'll later see. For now...

That partial lead slug removed from Denaro's cranium was a bit of a puzzler to the detectives on the case. They couldn't tell whether it was a .38 or a .45-caliber bullet. And they couldn't be blamed for that because it was only a fragment of a bullet.

The thought that it might have been fired from a .44-caliber revolver never entered anyone's mind, simply because .44s were in such rare supply and use in these parts.

Although the .44 Bulldog, as it's called, was manufactured by the Connecticut-based Charter Arms Company, it was still sold and used largely in the West, particularly Texas which in time shall figure with considerable prominence in the gruesome diary of the .44-caliber killer.

But a time came when the police belatedly determined that the caliber of the bullet which almost killed Denaro was indeed a .44. That happened not because of any excellence in the investigation's ranks but merely by the chance of accident—when Rosemary Keenan decided to spruce up her car a few days after the shooting.

"She found the other part of the slug while cleaning the car," Denaro revealed after he had joined the ranks of the officially recognized victims of the .44-caliber killer—four months later, in February.

"That's when she turned it over to detectives, who then established it was a .44 bullet."

The question was asked earlier: why would anyone want to shoot Carl Denaro?

"I guess when you think about it, all the elements were there for this guy," is how Denaro explained it. "My hair was dark brown and shoulder length. I was sitting on the passenger side of the car late at night, and he was looking at me from the rear.

"Of course I never caught a glimpse of the assailant. It was dark and I didn't exactly want to turn around to see what was coming my way."

After being placed on the list as one of the .44-caliber killer's victims, Denaro was asked if he held a grudge toward the madman.

"No," he replied. "I'm sure he's not in command of his senses. I just hope the police catch him soon so they can treat him for his illness."

The horror of his own experience at the hands of the .44-caliber killer didn't get to him, Denaro admitted, until the deadly night marauder struck for the fifth time in early March.

That was the killing of 19-year-old Columbia University coed Virginia Voskerichian of Forest Hills.

"That was a gruesome ordeal," Denaro said. "He just walked up to her and shot her in the face. When I heard that, it really got to me..."

CHAPTER VI

THE COLUMBIA COED
WAS ALONE

It got to a lot of other people, too. To Mayor Beame, to Police Commissioner Codd, but most significantly by then it had hit the entire city and churned a sea of fear from the tip of Coney Island to the far reaches of the Bronx, a twenty-six mile, fifty-cent subway ride.

The subway that figured in this episode, however wasn't the Brooklyn BMT or Bronx IRT, which together serve to link through a mid-Manhattan transfer point those two extremities of New York City. The underground rail line we're concerned with here is the IND which was Virginia Voskerichian's way of traveling between her home in Forest Hills and classes at Columbia University on Manhattan's Morningside Heights.

At nineteen, this pretty, brown-haired, brown-eyed young woman with the thin face and delicately chiseled features had everything to live for. She had come a long way since she and her family pulled up roots in Sophia, Bulgaria (where she was born) and settled in New York. That migration occurred December 16, 1968.

For Garabed Voskerichian, his adapted land proved good to him. He made a substantial living at his trade as a watchmaker. In time he moved his wife, Yolanda, and their three daughters and son into a splendid three-story brick home at 69-11 Exeter Street in a private preserve of 800 one-family houses and six cooperative apartments that is known as Forest Hills Gardens.

It is one of New York City's most prestigious communities and the homes with their stucco and Tudor-styled facades mirror the baronial splendor usually found only in the English countrysides. The community lies in the shadows of the West Side Tennis Club and famed Forest Hills Stadium where the celebrated tennis championships are played.

As Virginia grew up with her sisters and brother in that community, her warmth and conviviality gained her many friends. But while she was fun-loving and fancy-free, Virginia was also quite serious-minded as her 87% average at Forest Hills High School reflected. When she was graduated in 1974, she ranked 193rd in a class of 912.

Virginia had not yet made up her mind about what career she'd pursue, but she was certain that she wanted a higher education. So she enrolled as a Bachelor of Arts candidate at Queens College where her older sister, Alise, now twenty-seven, was soon to become a student teacher.

In 1975, Virginia, who had come to this country as a stateless person, fulfilled one of her fondest dreams. On July 29th of that year she became a naturalized citizen.

By the Fall of 1976, the college near her

home no longer sustained Virginia. She had made up her mind to major in Russian and Slavic cultures, languages, and literature, the studies she now decided were to shape her future as a translator and traveler. Thus she enrolled in the School of General Studies at Columbia's Barnard College, which has a high reputation for those studies. She very quickly proved to herself, to her professors, and fellow students that she had made the right choice of study.

When Virginia Voskerichian dropped into the university's Armenian Club after her last class that late afternoon of Tuesday, March 8th, she was on a cloud. She was bubbling over because she had just learned that her academic standing had risen to a scholarly 3.32 out of a possible 4.00—and she had made the Dean's List!

She stayed about forty minutes. Then Virginia bade goodnight to her friends at the club and left for home.

As a matter of unvarying routine, the 5 foot 6, 125 pound Virginia rode the IND subway between classes and home. That Tuesday night was apparently no different except in one respect; in rainy or chilly weather she took the bus from the Continental Avenue Station at Queens Boulevard to the stop just down the block from her home.

Though it was near freezing and blustery, we know now that Virginia did not precisely follow her accustomed mode of travel that Tuesday evening. She did not take the bus.

And the one person most concerned about Virginia Voskerichian that night and at that moment—her mother—knew then that she had decided to walk.

That was because Mrs. Voskerichian had been worried about her daughter. The rest of the family was home; they had waited with dinner for Virginia, but she had not returned punctually at 7 p.m.

Mrs. Voskerichian went to the corner of the living room at 7:15 and watched out the window for Virginia. The bus stop was almost across the street at Exeter Street and 69th Avenue.

It was getting very dark now. The minutes were passing painfully slow for Yolanda Voskerichian. Soon it was 8 p.m. Now she was really worried.

Even if Virginia had not taken the bus, the walk from the subway to the house shouldn't have taken any longer than five or six minutes. Unless Virginia had stopped on the way to talk to a friend. But, no, she wasn't insensitive to the other members of her family. She would know they were waiting for her and she wouldn't tarry. She'd walk directly home.

It certainly was in her mother's mind that Virginia's path home was not the most ideal for night strollers. The six blocks she had to walk along Continental Avenue were safe enough since they were brightly lighted and were heavily traveled. But once she turned into Dartmouth Street where Forest Hills

Gardens begins, the streets are poorly lit. Lampposts have such low-wattage bulbs that the area looks more like something in the gaslight era rather than a period nearly a century after Edison gave light to the world.

Then, too, Mrs. Voskerichian couldn't erase from her mind the horrible memory of last January 30th, barely more than a month past. It had happened almost around the corner in Station Square and hundreds of other residents besides Mrs. Voskerichian had become everlastingly fearful after Christine Freund's mysterious murder.

The deep concern that had grown inside Mrs. Voskerichian that night of March 8th was soon to explode into palpable shock and terror.

Mrs. Voskerichian was still standing in the corner of the living room looking out the window at a few minutes past eight when all at once she saw a familiar figure—a woman who lived in the neighborhood—approaching the house with quick, urgent steps.

She stopped abruptly at the front door and rang the bell with alarming insistency.

Her heart pounding now, Mrs. Voskerichian went to the foyer on leaden feet and opened the door.

"Your daughter fainted," the woman said breathlessly. "They are taking her to the hospital..."

"Where...how?" a voice from inside the house was heard.

Slender, bearded Dikran Voskerichian

surged toward the door.

"She is lying on the ground by the entrance on Dartmouth Street," the woman gasped.

Dikran brushed past his mother and the woman and took off at a full sprint for that destination, two and a half blocks away.

When he reached the scene in front of the apartment building at No. 4 Dartmouth, Dikran saw the crowd and blue policemen's uniforms. Then he glimpsed through an opening in the circle of people looking down on the form of a young woman lying outstretched and Dikran Voskerichian suddenly went limp.

He recognized the Paris-styled Winter jacket, the peasant skirt, and knee-high, high-heeled beige leather boots. Next to the body he saw the books his sister had carried to school with her that morning. There was a hole through the books that police ballistics experts would later identify as having been shaped by the penetration of a bullet—a bullet that the books couldn't stop.

Next to the books on the sidewalk was an ominous stream of blood that was flowing from the region of the head. Dikran could not see where exactly the wound was but, as he would later learn, the bullet that passed through the books also plowed into Virginia's mouth. It not only shattered several of her teeth but tore through her head and lodged in her cranium near the spinal cord.

She had died instantly.

"Virginia...Virginia..." Dikran began

sobbing. A patrolman and several neighbors tried to console and comfort him.

Even now in the crowd the disturbing voice of doom rose in a crescendo. Soon fear and near-panic would grip the community where bankers and lawyers and others with stature and affluence live in homes with cut-stone and stuccoed fronts, gabled roofs, and those additional distinctive architectural adornments which escalate valuations above a minimum base of $100,000 per dwelling.

Everyone in this enclave of easy circumstance had thought, for ever so long, that the community was safe from the violent crimes that plagued so many other sections of the city. That is, they did—until Christine Freund was murdered. There were still many even after that who viewed the crime as an isolated case, that it would not happen again.

But now it had—just a half block away. The neighborhood was scared to death. And justifiably so, because the police were apparently so thoroughly bewildered and befuddled by this killing and its motive as they had been in each of the previous four mysterious attacks.

It would be several hours before homicide detectives from the 15th Zone would learn that the bullet which killed Virginia Voskerichian was a .44-caliber. That information would follow the removal of the fatal slug during the autopsy by Dr. Jacques Durosier, Queens County assistant medical examiner.

Meanwhile, Captain Joseph Borrelli, chief

of Queens homicide, deployed 100 detectives to the area in a move that obviously anticipated what was soon to come from City Hall and Police Headquarters.

The early phase of the investigation at the scene turned up an elderly man who offered a partial picture of what had happened. He told detectives that he was walking home at about 7:30 to 7:40 p.m. when he heard a "pop" that he surmised was a fire-cracker exploding.

A second or two later, he said, he saw a white youth who looked to be in his late teens or early twenties running toward him. As he drew closer, he pulled a knitted dark-colored stocking cap down over his face.

"On passing me," the man told detectives, "I heard him saying, 'Oh, Jesus!' But I had no idea what he could have meant—until I learned that the young girl was murdered. He must have been disturbed that I had seen his face..."

The witness said the young man was about 160 pounds, 5 feet 8, and was wearing dark trousers and a dark waist-length coat.

Another passerby, a youth of nineteen, unaware of either the shot fired or the presence of the stocking-capped young man fleeing the area, almost tripped over the girl's body as he rounded the corner from Continental Avenue, en route to his home on Exeter.

The force of the bullet evidently had catapulted the victim's body, head forward, into the base of a row of overgrown evergreens alongside the apartment house. Her legs, however, had remained stretched on the sidewalk.

The young man caught himself from falling and quickly attempted to play the role of a Good Samaritan. He kneeled, turned the girl over, and was about to try reviving her with mouth-to-mouth resuscitation. But then he saw the blood trickling from her mouth and realized he couldn't help. He ran to a police call box and reported his grim find.

The search for clues and evidence at the scene was an exercise in frustration. For, other than the books with the bullet hole through them, there was nothing to tell police anything about the crime.

But later when the school texts were analyzed by the lab sleuths, that evidence would show a heavy concentration of burned gunpowder residue. And that told police the killer had fired at his victim at very close range—no more than two or three feet.

To detectives that meant Virginia evidently had seen her killer approaching and raised the books to her head in a vain attempt to fend off the fatal bullet.

Detectives went to Virginia's home to question the family. Her brother acted as interpreter for his parents and spokesman in general for the family. He assured authorities that his sister had no enemies, that he knew of no one who'd want to harm her. Except...

"It must be that crazy man who killed that other girl," Dikran said, referring to Christine Freund's motiveless killing that had happened barely 300 yards from where his sister was shot to death.

Dikran, who made his living working in an auto parts store in Glendale, Queens, also had the heart-breaking task of returning home and telling his family what had happened to Virginia.

Later, after detectives left, he made a vow: "I'm going to get even. I'm never going to rest until my sister's killer is caught."

"I've got to get even. I can't go through life without doing something about this...I'm freaking out. I'm going to get even with that lunatic."

Then Dikran nodded at the door through which the detectives had recently gone out.

"The stupid police waste their time going after kids smoking marijuana while they let shmucks like this run around loose. I know it's the same guy who shot that other girl two months ago. It's got to be. I just know it."

Dikran gazed across the room for a long moment. Now his face grew dark.

"I saw my sister lying there in her own blood," he stammered in anger. "Her textbooks were next to her. They had a bullet hole in them, like she knew what was about to happen. I just hope she didn't suffer too much..."

Tears welled in the young man's eyes now. He was unable to control his emotions and he punched on the furniture around him.

"I'm going to get even," he promised once more, now sobbing. "Because what bothers me is that the scum who did this may get away. But I won't let him."

A moment later Mrs. Voskerichian turned to Virginia's sister, "Alise," she commanded in her native Armenian, "Go pick out the dress for Virginia. Pick out the one she liked best and we will give it to the undertaker..."

As the family made preparations for Virginia's funeral, the search for the killer and the investigation went on.

By the next day, the whole complexion of the inquiry took on a different tone. For the boys at the lab had suddenly discovered— once the bullet taken from Virginia's head had been examined—that the barrel riflings were the same as those on the slug that had killed Christine Freund.

With startling swiftness now, the lab men took everything off the back burners. And that covered a multitude of results of tests on .44-caliber bullets—those that killed Donna Lauria and wounded Jody Valente, as well as the findings from examination of the slug that struck Carl Denaro in the head on that unheralded October night attack in Flushing. The resolutions reached as well on the examination of bullets from the Donna DeMasi-Joanne Lomino shootings.

The cops had suddenly come to realize that all the bullets delivered to the lab over all those months after all those shootings—had been fired from the same .44-caliber revolver!

Chapin once said: "Through every rift of discovery some seeming anomaly drops out of the darkness, and falls, as a golden link, into the great chain of order."

Now indeed light had replaced darkness and the links were all in place in the great chain of the investigation. Now at long last the police knew exactly what was going on.

Now without question the police accepted as absolute fact that a murderous assassin was on the loose. It certainly wasn't the first instance that a terrorist roamed the city's streets. Yet never was New York confronted with the awesome presence of an apparently psychopathic gunman such as this.

Moreover, never had the police of this city taken so long to recognize a menace of such magnitude—even when they had composite drawings and the hard evidence of the identical bullet markings under their very noses all the time.

The police also drew some other obvious conclusions, such as that all the .44-caliber killer's victims were cast from an almost identical mould from the standpoint of appearance. They, all of them, had long, dark brown hair, hair that fell shoulder-length in every case—even Carl Denaro's. Most probably he had been mistaken from behind as a girl, not only because of his long hair but also because he was sitting on the passenger side of the car.

Now that police and the public had full awareness about the stalking night killer, certain questions followed naturally.

Who was this maniacal gunman? Why was

he killing and wounding by the numbers? How were police going to track him down before he struck again? What particular fascination or hatred possessed him to murder and maim only people with long, brown hair?

Those questions were asked over and over but they repeatedly and unvaryingly defied any answers.

The last thing Mayor Beame wanted was to alarm the people of his city. Yet now there was that ominous and awesome presence of an obviously psychopathic gunman with a proven killer complex. The Mayor and Police Commissioner sensed their duty and obligation to the city's nearly 8,000,000 residents about the great menace.

"We have a savage killer on the loose," Beame adm_____ sombre voice at a press conference that he and Codd had called in the Flushing police station after the laboratory had linked Virginia Voskerichian's killing to the other cases.

"He is singling out women with shoulder-length dark brown hair. We don't know why..."

Codd also offered that the approximate description of the twisted killer was that of a white male, 25 to 30 years old, of medium build in the height range of 5 feet 10 to 6 feet, had dark brown hair combed straight back, and was well groomed.

Beame then urged the public to come forward with any information they might have on anyone they suspected could fit the killer's pedigree.

"Don't use your judgment as to whether what you have is important or not," the Mayor implored. "Just come forward and tell police."

A special police number was established: 520-9200.

"All New Yorkers have been shocked," the Mayor declared further at the news conference. "We must do all we can to stop these senseless murders."

Codd then disclosed that the same gun had been used in the five attacks which so far had claimed three lives and wounded four.

As the investigation into her murder was continued with a full force of detectives, Virginia Voskerichian's last rites were held on that Saturday in the Edward D. Jamie Funeral Chapel at 141-26 Northern Boulevard in Flushing. More than two-hundred mourners overflowed the chapel for the final tribute to Virginia. The service was followed with interment in Kew Gardens' Maple Grove Cemetery.

Meanwhile, as a result of Mayor Beame's plea for the public's assistance, the phones at the 520-9200 switchboard in the Flushing stationhouse jangled incessantly.

"It's a trememdous response," said Captain Borrelli. "The phones haven't stopped ringing. All the calls are being followed up."

Borrelli said that his detectives were poring over every shred of evidence that was before them.

"We are looking for any hint of rhyme or

reason for the killings," he explained. "So far we haven't come up with one, but we're continuing to search for the answer. We want this guy before he strikes again."

A week went by and again Borrelli was asked to report on the progress of the investigation.

"We've had more than three-hundred tips phoned in to the Queens Detective Area at the 520-9200 phone, but so far none has panned out," he admitted.

"We have reached most of the people who called in and we're still running down other tips, but we haven't really gotten anything that would make you perk up and say, 'Hey, that looks pretty good.'

"Chasing this guy is like chasing a shadow. So far as we can see the killer is faceless..."

Yet that wasn't exactly true because sketches of the killer had already been worked up by the police department after his attacks on Donna Lauria and Jody Valente and again after Donna DeMasi and Joanne Lomino were shot by him.

The police had three sets of sketches; the first was made July 30, 1976, on information and detail supplied by Jody Valente; a second sketch was drawn after the November 27th attack in Floral Park with a description provided by Donna DeMasi; and a third was pencilled on the recollection of Joanne Lomino. Three sketches that now, in retrospect, could have alerted the public, as sketches of fugitives are expected to. At least the first

one—showing a man with a wide face and a
nose whose tip seemed slightly pinched, eyes
that had a cold, steely look, and brown, curly
or somewhat crinkly hair—may have helped
joggle some memories if it had been released
then and not months later as part of a package
of sketches.

Why the police held back on those three
early sketches is one of the lingering myster-
ies of the investigation. In fact, it wasn't until
March 16th that they did anything about
alerting the public to the fugitive killer's
appearance. That was the day they released
two composite sketches of the man who shot
Virginia Voskerichian. One of them had a
startling resemblance to the drawing made on
Jody Valente's information.

And why we keep harping on that first
sketch is that it—and the one just
mentioned—both have an astonishing likeness to the face on the cover of this book, that
of the man authorities finally captured as the
alleged .44-caliber killer.

But in the final analysis the sketches were
all put before the public and no one could
identify the .44-caliber killer. It is unlikely
that with the fleeting, terror-stricken glimpses
the victims got of the killer, even Leonardo
daVinci would have been hard-pressed to
come up with a more accurate likeness of the
fugitive. So no criticism is intended here for
the NYPD's dedicated artists. It's only directed against the sluggish and sloppy handling
of the sketches by the department in that early

period that fault is found by us.

The investigation into Virginia Voskerichian's murder was obviously getting nowhere, yet there were some stirrings. For example, Detectives Martin Hopkins and John O'Connell took in custody a 31-year-old Queens man and charged him with having thirteen unlicensed pistols and rifles in his possession—one of them the rare .44-caliber revolver which had been used in the series of murders and shootings. But the gun owned by Donald Smith, of 71-57 Metropolitan Avenue in Glendale, Queens, was not the one in the killings.

Described as an out-of-work security guard, Smith was arrested in a Ridgewood bar after an anonymous tip in response to Mayor Beame's appeal to the public. Hopkins and O'Connell arrested Smith after they spotted him in the tavern with the butt of a .25-caliber revolver sticking out of his belt. The detectives also searched the suspect's apartment and found seven more pistols, including the .44, and six rifles.

Smith told police he belonged to a local gun club and that he had been a big game hunter. He showed the sleuths pictures of himself in Africa.

Smith was booked for possessing dangerous weapons, was held overnight for arraignment in Queens Criminal Court. But, then in the morning, Assistant District Attorney Martin Bracken let it be known that Smith was a harmless character and that the charges against him would not be pursued.

Because of the investigative standstill in Virginia Voskerichian's killing—and in all the other shootings in Queens and the Bronx attributed to the .44-caliber killing—the Forest Hills community felt it had sufficient cause to hold a protest rally.

Several hundred dwellers from the beleaguered area responded to the call of the meeting on Monday night, March 21st, in Public School 144 at 69th Avenue and Kessel Street.

Fear had been growing in Forest Hills since the last murder and it was at peak now.

"We are here to demonstrate our concern for safety in the streets," said Joseph DeVoy, president of the Forest Hills Community Association, a homeowners' group representing nine hundred families.

"They have given us extra police and we want to make sure they stay."

City Councilman Arthur J. Katzman, who organized the meeting, said, "The plea that this is a low-crime area just doesn't address the question of why we don't have more police on our streets. The community demands protection."

Urging the residents to write to the Mayor and Police Commissioner, Katzman then echoed what DeVoy had asked for—continued protection for the Forest Hills area. But a large group in the audience kept shouting and interrupting the introductions and the speakers as well. They felt compelled to cry out against what they believe to be inadequate representation for them.

"We didn't come here tonight to hear the politicians," one man in the audience shouted denouncingly. "We want to know what's going on with the case. Are the newspaper stories accurate? How can we as private citizens help?"

The answers didn't come out of that meeting. But in time an answer did come. The newspaper accounts about the .44-caliber killer were quite accurate. He was indeed the city's most vicious and violent killer of all time. The expressions of fear that he could strike again were not idle ones. Because the time wasn't too far off when he'd again leave his lethal calling card...

CHAPTER VII

THEY STOPPED TO SMOOCH

It happened in a parked car once again.

A car parked on the service road of the Bronx's Hutchinson River Parkway about a block from Valentina Suriani's home at 1950 Hutchinson—and only two blocks from the scene of the .44-caliber killer's first ambushing which killed Donna Lauria and wounded Jody Valente.

Pretty, dark-haired nineteen-year-old Valentina, or Valerie as all her friends called her, was in many ways a mix or an amalgam of some of the other girls we've spoken about in this narrative who've faced the .44-caliber killer.

Like Virginia Voskerichian, Valerie Suriani was a college coed. But she wasn't into studies like Virginia was. Valerie was a well-liked, low-key undergraduate at Lehman College in the North Bronx where she was studying acting.

That isn't to say Miss Suriani couldn't have made the Dean's Lists and other honors. After all, her academic achievements at St. Lucy's Grammar School enabled her to enter St. Catherine's Academy with such superb scholastic preparation that she went the route to graduation in the three-year accelerated program.

Getting a good well-rounded education was a necessity to Valerie. But becoming an actress, well, that was a burning obsession. Yet, she harbored just the slightest bit of apprehension about that career because, as Valerie had confided in a number of friends, she was thinking of chucking her studies at Lehman College and taking courses at the Fashion Institute of Technology in the Garment District downtown. Virginia Voskerichian also had changed her mind as she matured at Queens College and switched to Columbia.

Like her neighbor, Donna Lauria, whom she did not know, Valentina, or Valerie, had an abiding love for animals. Donna had a real dog and oodles of stuffed animals while Valerie prized stray cats as pets—and also tended to injured animals in the street.

Christine Freund and John Diel have talked and planned marriage for seven years. Valentina Suriani and her twenty-year-old steady, Alexander Esau, had been making such similar plans for three years. They had both talked about marriage but Valerie and Sandy, as friends called him, never got around to setting a date.

Even Valerie and Sandy, themselves, couldn't explain exactly why they hadn't gone beyond the talking stage about matrimony. But then they both had plans about their respective careers that intruded to a degree on any serious steps they might have wanted to take toward marriage.

For Sandy, a graduate of Brooklyn Technical High School, college was not a goal. At least not for the present. Even his job as tow-truck driver for the Luna Brothers Towing Company at 532 West 46th Street in Manhattan was a temporary arrangement.

Working there was a living and it was a convenience as well. It was only a short distance from the fourth-floor walkup he shared with his father, Rudolph, at 352 West 46th Street, where a concentration of some of the city's better known eating establishments have given the block the label of *Restaurant Row*.

What held fascination and promise of better things for Sandy was his contemplated enlistment in the Coast Guard. He had an irresistible attraction to the sea and, coupled with his mechanical proclivity, he gathered that he could go a long way in that branch of service.

It was neither unexpected nor surprising that Alexander Esau should have exhibited technical skills because in his growing-up years in that Hell's Kitchen neighborhood he was always tinkering with model cars and electric trains.

In recent years, understandably, Sandy Esau had turned his attentions to another interest...

Valerie Suriani was a vivacious, fun-loving young woman who seemed to complement her beau so well that those who watched them together, scooting about the shops and restaurants and movies in the Baychester area, all agreed they made a charming couple.

Just as on any other Friday after work that April 18th evening, Alexander Esau went home, washed, dressed, and drove to the Bronx. After parking his 1969 maroon Mercury Montego near the thirteen-story red-brick apartment building, Esau rode the elevator to the twelfth floor and found Valentina, alerted by his buzzing from the lobby, waiting at the open door.

He entered and greeted Valentina's parents, Frank and Maria Suriani, who'd been living in the five-room apartment for some five years now, after having moved from an East Bronx neighborhood that was beginning to be invaded by those torch-bearing savages we spoke of earlier. Another daughter, Nancy, was also a member of the family. But she had moved out a few months before after she had married.

"Where are you going tonight?" smiled Mrs. Suriani.

"To the movies, ma," Valerie trilled. Then she took Sandy's hand and said, "Come on, or we'll be late..."

It was 9 p.m. when the couple disappeared out the door.

It was a little after 4 o'clock the next morning when Mr. and Mrs. Suriani were awakened from bed by detectives who had brought them the grievous news about their daughter's death.

It happened in the parked car in front of one of a row of red brick and clapboard two-story one-family detached homes on the tree-lined Hutchinson River Parkway service road. The number of the house in front of where the couple had parked was 1878 but that holds no significance other than it's just down the street—only six houses away—from where the Surianis lived.

Valerie and Sandy apparently parked there because it was the only vacancy at the curb. Space is at premium in that neighborhood at night because the apartment dwellers spurn costly garage space in their own buildings for free curbside parking.

Their arrival there sometime before 3 a.m. of that Saturday followed a brief stop by Esau at a bachelor party in his girlfriend's neighborhood. He'd left Valentina in the car because he was merely paying a token visit at the party simply to convey his best wishes to the groom-to-be.

"Where's Valerie?" asked Joseph Madden, a close friend and co-worker with Sandy at the towing company.

"Out in the car," replied Esau, explaining that he had dropped in to wish the guest of honor well.

"We're going to cruise around the neighborhood, Val and I."

Then Esau left and drove away with his sweetheart, eventually finding that spot to park and, who really knows, perhaps to smooch a bit.

It was 3 a.m. now and a resident in one of the homes heard four explosions that he recognized immediately as gunfire. He dialed the police.

Uniformed officers responded in radio cruisers and found what would soon be acknowledged as the .44-caliber killer's eighth and ninth victims.

Miss Suriani, seated on the passenger side, had been struck by a bullet in the head and was beyond aid. Esau, behind the wheel, had been struck by three of the bullets, all in the head. Yet, incredibly, he was still alive although unconscious.

The killer had apparently leaped from the shadows in front of the car and fired through the windshield, which was shattered.

As Esau was removed from the car and rushed by ambulance to Jacobi Hospital for surgery, detectives turned up the first significant evidence since the .44-caliber killer's rampage had begun the previous Summer.

It was in an envelope lying on the seat beside Miss Suriani's body. The block lettering on the envelope had Captain Joseph Borrelli's name. Detectives who opened the envelope found a four-sheet letter written to the chief of Queens Homicide.

With care not to smudge or obliterate any finger or palm prints the writer might have left on the pages, the detectives gingerly unfolded the letter and read the message, written in a uniquely-styled block letter format characterized by remarkably uniform slantings of the seriffs at 45-degree angles. The lettering looked very much as though the scrivener might be a cartoonist.

The police would not divulge the message and it would be four months more before the contents were known—published exclusively in the *New York Post* after star investigative reporter Carl Pelleck obtained a copy from "a source," as he put it, "that I won't reveal if they put my neck under the guillotine."

The letter read:

"I am deeply hurt by your calling me a wemon (sic) hater. I am not. But I am a monster.

"I am the 'Son of Sam.' I am a little 'brat.'

"When father Sam gets drunk he gets mean. He beats his family. Sometimes he ties me up to the back of the house. Other times he locks me in the garage. Sam loves to drink blood.

"'Go out and kill' commands father Sam.

"Behind our house some rest. Mostly young—raped and slaughtered—their blood drained—just bones now.

"Papa Sam keeps me locked in the attic, too. I can't get out but I look out the attic window and watch the world go by.

"I feel like an outsider. I am on a different wavelength then (sic) everybody else—programmed too (sic) kill.

"However, to stop me you must kill me. Attention all police: Shoot me first—shoot to kill or else keep out of my way or you will die!

"Papa Sam is old now. He needs some blood to preserve his youth. He has had too many heart attacks. Too many heart attacks. 'Ugh, me hoot it hurts sonny boy.'

"I miss my pretty princess most of all. She's resting in our ladies house. But I'll see her soon.

"I am the 'Monster'—'Beelzebub'—the chubby behemouth(sic).

"I love to hunt. Prowling the streets looking for fair game—tasty meat. The wemon(sic) of Queens are prettyist (sic) of all. I must be the water they drink. I live for the hunt—my life. Blood for papa.

"Mr. Borelli (sic), sir, I don't want to kill anymore. No sir, no more but I must, 'honour thy father.'

"I want to make love to the world. I love people. I don't belong on earth. Return me to yahoos.

"To the people of Queens, I love you. And I [the letter 'M' was crossed out] want to wish all of you a happy Easter. May God bless you in this life and in the next. And for now I say goodbye and goodnight.

"POLICE: Let me haunt you with these words:

"I'll be back!

"I'll be back!

"To be interrpreted (sic) as—bang,

bang, bang, bank (sic), bang—'ugh!!'
"Yours in murder
"'Mr. Monster'"

Much of what "Mr. Monster" wrote in the letter was dismissed by police as incomprehensible gibberish. Yet there were a number of passages that they certainly must have understood—and very clearly, too. Such as the next to last two sentences where the writer vowed, "I'll be back! I'll be back!"

Chief of Detectives John Keenan let it be known that "There is nothing in the letter to indicate any reason for these killings...I can't say anymore about the note because could prove to be a very important piece evidence after we've captured this mad-an."

That decision to withhold the contents of the letter from the public may not have been the wisest strategy. For as we'll see in time, a man named Sam really existed—though not in quite the same image as the .44-caliber killer described him in his note. But had this letter been published in the newspapers, it is conceivable that the Sam referred to might have recognized the references to him—and been able to alert police to the identity of the letter writer.

Though the letter was withheld by police, it shall remain to the everlasting credit of the *New York Daily News* and the perceptive reporters with talent on the staff that one of the key phrases saw the light of day immediately. William Federici scooped the city by busting the story in his newspaper's April 19th editions that the handwritten note taunted the police and warned "I'll do it again."

The story also reported that the killer "lives in a nightmare world where he sees bloodsucking vampires and Frankenstein monsters."

Even the *National Enquirer* and *Midnight* didn't go that route. But since the story was written by Paul Meskil we shouldn't blame Federici for that line which very obviously was, as we say in the trade, a "pipe job."

In the late editions of the *New York Times* of that same day, Deputy Police Commissioner Francis J. McLoughlin, the press liaison was reported to have denied the *Daily News* story that the murderer had said in his note, "I'll do it again."

That seemed to be a very indelicate thing for McLoughlin to have done since he had once worked as a reporter for the *News*. But as so many of his predecessors in the job, all of them ex-reporters on the city's newspapers, McLoughlin apparently surrendered his own principles as a journalist and adapted the covert smugness and deceptiveness of a public relations *flack*.

If Frank, in all honesty, can differentiate between "I'll do it again" and "I'll be back!" and, moreover, if he can say the letter didn't in effect promise more killings, then I would like to hear it.

The investigation at the scene, conducted under the direction of Captain Stephen Kelly of the Bronx Area Detective Squad, turned up no other clues aside from the letter.

The letter itself was delivered to the laboratory detectives when they arrived on the scene and it was taken downtown, envelope and all, for analysis. It was found to contain several clear-impression fingerprints as well as one palm print. This evidence was turned over immediately to the Bureau of Criminal Investigation. To jump ahead, nothing popped up on those prints.

For that we should not put down the NYPD nor FBI, since the man subsequently seized as the .44-caliber killer didn't have a police record. But as for the military—the U.S. Army in particular—well, is it fair to condemn that branch of the service for not identifying the finger and palm prints of the .44-caliber killer from its records of his service?

Certainly not—especially since no one in the NYPD had asked the military to run a checkout on those prints. But that doesn't reflect any dereliction of duty. It's simply that, we're told, the "state of the art" in the science of fingerprint detection and identification hasn't reached that stage when prints off paper can be used to retrieve matching prints on file.

Such prints, police officials insisted, can

only serve for identification purposes when the suspect is in custody, his prints are taken on the spot, and then a comparison is made.

That technicality aside, one would still think that so far the cops didn't really want to solve the .44-caliber killer's murderous rampages and capture the SOB. But that wasn't the case at all. It was just that the NYPD can suffer lapses just as any organization run by average, normal humans can.

The trackdown of the killer was still disjointed. Cops in Queens searching, cops in the Bronx on the prowl. To some extent, it can be said, they were even tripping over each other in their efforts to unearth clues and evidence. And they were getting nowhere in the process.

"There appears to be a direct link between the other shootings of the .44-caliber victims and the case we have here," asserted Lieutenant John Powers of the 8th Homicide Zone in the Bronx.

That was probably the truest statement any cop had made on the case in the eight months that the madman was on his frenzied venture. But Powers' voice was not fated to echo much longer for the powers on high were descending on the borough of the Bronx to impose their supreme and overriding authority.

"We're calling on Queens homicide detectives to assist in the investigation," declared Chief Keenan for openers. "That's in the neighborhood of fifty men, including every available detective in the Bronx."

Now at last the NYPD was beginning to show the first semblances of organization and motivation to move with expediency and efficiency to capture the .44-caliber killer.

At Jacobi Hospital, meanwhile, Rudolf Esau held a tearful vigil at his son's bedside in the intensive care unit following the delicate brain surgery which had been performed by a team of doctors, including one of the country's most highly-esteemed neurosurgeons.

But the watch at his son's bedside was soon to end in shattering disillusionment for the father. Because some eighteen hours after he had been brought to the hospital—at 9:38 p.m. Sunday—Alexander Esau became the .44-caliber killer's fifth fatality.

As Esau went off to prepare for his son's neral, the services for Valentina Suriani gan on that Wednesday morning. The mourners gathered in the sunshine outside St. Theresa's Church in the Baychester area and spoke of their love and adoration for Valerie.

When services in the church began, the priest, the principal celebrant of the funeral Mass, the Rev. Francis Oliverio, of St. Lucy's Church, said: "I know your hearts are broken, yet I want you to hear me out. Your daughter is not gone..."

He was addressing his remarks to Valentina's parents and family, including a grey-haired grandmother who was in the front pew.

"Val is home with God," the priest intoned. "If that weren't so, God would be just as deranged as those who do these acts."

The casket was then carried out of the church on the shoulders of six pallbearers in gray-striped trousers and placed in the hearse for the final ride to the cemetery...

Alexander Esau's last rites were held the next morning at the Failla Funeral Home in North Bergen, across the Hudson River from Manhattan, in New Jersey.

There's one short last chapter to write here about this young man's last moments in the hospital. His mother, Ingrid, who was separated from her husband, Rudolph, had come to the hospital for the death watch, too.

And she also gave her consent for the removal of Sandy's kidneys and corneas for transplantation. That permission was obtained from Mrs. Esau at 8 p.m. when all hope for survival was gone. An hour and a half later, young Esau was dead—but his organs were preserved to help others...

"We have some tips and some possibilities," Chief Keenan offered. "But there is no suspect who is a real hot possibility..."

Increasingly, Chief Keenan's voice was being heard now, above all the other commanders of Queens and Bronx detective forces.

That was an augury of things soon to come—when the investigation of the .44-caliber killer's heinous crimes was to come under a unified command headed by one boss. The time for that strategic departure was but hours away now...

CHAPTER VIII

POLICE TASK FORCE: "WE'RE GOING TO GET THIS GUY!"

The .44-caliber killer, or Son of Sam or Mr. Monster as he called himself, had been having a distinct advantage over the police up to that April 19th when Police Commissioner Codd made his long-overdue move and established a unified command in search for the mad murderer.

It was about time, too, for the man with the twisted, tortured mind and the big cannon with the hand grip could roam like a jackal in search of prey. He was not committed to observe the restrictions of borough commands and squad jurisdictions, as his hunters were required to do.

The killer's search for victims to provide "some blood to preserve" Sam's youth was unhindered. He could prowl the streets "looking for fair game—tasty meat"—anywhere he wanted.

So far he'd struck a half-dozen times in two of the city's five boroughs—twice in the Bronx, four times in Queens. Yet none of the investigations, conducted for the most part by different sets of detectives, had led the police one short step closer to the killer.

They were, on that April 19th, as ignorant

about his identity, as hopelessly unaware of his whereabouts, and as grievously unknowing of when he would strike again as they had been from the moment Donna Lauria and Jody Valente were gunned down in the Bronx nine months earlier on July 29th of 1976. Of course, there'd been great leads. Moments when the investigation in one or another of the killings or woundings had given the sleuths hope and heart. But always the inevitable letdown followed.

In the beginning, it can be said that no one on the investigation considered the possibility that a fiend, parched with a thirst to kill and maim innocent young women, had struck down Donna and Jody. If anything, it seemed to Detectives Richard Paul and Ronald Denison that the shooting echoed a possible revenge motive. That angle loomed with particular promise when the probers learned that one of the girls had a falling out with a boyfriend who had taken off for New Mexico after the shooting.

Paul, together with Detective Charles Summers, took a plane to Albuquerque and nosed around. They soon found that the object of their inquiry was staying in a locale where a .44-caliber revolver had been bought a while back—by a man who once lived a mere six blocks from Buhre Avenue where Donna and Jody were gunned down. With an assist from New Mexico authorities, the .44 was traced and test fired. It wasn't the gun which had triggered the bullets in the Bronx.

Of course, when Paul and Summers returned home and reported their findings to their superiors, nobody then suggested a psycho could have been crouched behind the barrel of that gun which killed Donna and wounded Jody.

Three months later when Carl Denaro was shot in Flushing while seated beside Rosemary Keenan, a similar futile search for an assailant ensued.

There was a damn good reason that Detective Redman Keenan of the Flushing Squad wanted to solve that shooting. Because the girl behind the wheel of that Volkswagen who escaped injury was none other than the eldest of his five daughters!

Keenan was asleep at home in Breezy Point on Long Island when Rosemary phoned from Peck's Pub after alerting the friends inside to the fact that Carl was bleeding and unconscious in the car. She didn't know her boyfriend had been shot. She thought a vandal had smashed the car's window and that the blood on Denaro's head was inflicted by flying glass.

Even the cops on the scene thought that was the case until they learned differently from the doctor who took the partial .44-caliber slug from Carl's head and put a metal plate in place to protect the area where the bone was shattered.

In what is probably one of the more outstanding ironies in the saga of Son of Sam's depredations, Detective Keenan was assigned to investigate the case. In the routine of squad operations, it was his turn to "catch the squeal."

Once he learned that the guy with Rosemary had been shot and not hurt by something thrown by a vandal, Keenan backed his daughter into a corner and pumped her for an explanation.

"Has this anything to do with you and Carl?" he demanded.

"Anything like drugs involved?"

"Tell me the truth...nobody gets shot without a reason..."

Over and over the questions were asked. Rosemary was beside herself. She swore she was telling the truth. Keenan still harbored doubts. He reverted to the old "good guy-bad guy" routine that the cops still keep pulling. He sent another detective to cajole, console and then ask her, "Is there something you want to tell me that you can't tell your father?"

Meanwhile, Keenan also quizzed Denaro without letup. He, too, was as adamant as Rosemary. He couldn't come up with any reason that he or the detective's daughter should be shot.

In a grasp at straws, Keenan hit Motor Vehicle Bureau records for blue Volkswagens like the one his daughter drove. If he could find someone else with such a car in the neighborhood, then maybe he could prove a case of mistaken identity.

He got nowhere with that tack.

But then, many, many weeks later, a ballistics detective, George Simmons, got to talking with Keenan and told him about the lab having done studies on some .44-caliber bullets that went downtown from a Bronx shooting in late July. Not long after, Detective Bernard Judge, from the Bellerose Squad, informed Keenan about .44-bullets having been fired in the third random shooting, of Joanne Lomino and Donna DeMasi.

By then Detective Redman Keenan knew what the police brass refused to recognize—at least publicly—until at least one more young woman, Christine Freund, was gunned down and killed.

The fact that Keenan's daughter was the girl in the driver's seat beside Denaro that October night was kept a closely guarded secret. Not even the detectives who worked beside Keenan were aware of the relationship. Keenan, himself, was to be recruited shortly for duty with the newly-formed Task Force. He would be assigned to the 15th Homicide Zone and put in charge of a team that searched for the source of the .44-caliber killer's gun and ammunition. It was a search that led nowhere, just as so many other ventures of the Task Force were fated to lead.

Commissioner Codd decided, after suggestions from Chief Keenan (no relation to the detective), from Captain Borrelli, and other bosses from both the Bronx and Queens, to establish a command post for the Task Force in the 109th Precinct in Flushing. This modern two-story building is a far cry from the majority of the NYPD's aging, rickety station houses throughout the city. It stands hard by Shea Stadium where the Jets and Mets do seasonal battle in football and baseball.

A "war room" was installed on the second floor in Room 224. The man given command with thirty crack operatives wasted little time preparing this headquarters for deployment of his troops and the battle with the phantom killer.

The man Codd picked to lead the search for the .44-caliber killer was a serene, soft-spoken 61-year-old 37-year veteran who stood nearly 6 feet tall with slender features and a face that could very well have been a parish priest's. Deputy Inspector Timothy J. Dowd might also have chosen the way of the cloth, for he'd been born in Ireland. Dowd had emigrated as a child with his parents to Boston and grew up there. He then moved to New York and enrolled at City College where he earned a B.A. degree in literature and Latin and a degree in public administration from Bernard M. Baruch College.

Then, incongruously, he took the exam for policeman and made it in 1940. While Latin didn't help him as he pounded his first beat in Harlem, at least it provided him with some understanding on Sundays during Mass.

His rise in the department was meteoric. By the mid-1960's Dowd was commanding the

10th District Detectives in Brooklyn. By 1973, he was Inspector Timothy J. Dowd—but there was trouble ahead.

The then Police Commissioner Donald Cawley had gone on a shape-up-or-ship-out kick with his top commanders, demanding greater productivity at the pain of perishment.

Dowd was one of fifteen veteran commanders busted; he was reduced to captain. But while most of the beleaguered gold braid simply retired rather than take demotions, Dowd and four other officers decided to fight. They took their cases to the State Human Rights Commission. Their key argument was that they were being discriminated against because of age. Dowd was 58 at the time.

A year later Cawley had gone the route of commissioners who make too many waves and Michael Codd took the helm. He threw a life preserver to Dowd after a little egging from the Human Rights people. Dowd's rank was restored and he was sent into the field where he performed with excellence.

When the .44-caliber killer was beginning to leave his imprint of terror in the outer boroughs, Dowd was deeply involved in the investigation of extortion rackets in Chinatown. By February he had smashed the plot and arrested the murderous leader of the Flying Dragons.

Dowd was now free to take another assignment; it was one of the biggest that could go to any policeman:

Catch Son of Sam!

Very soon after installing himself in the second-floor "war room" of the Flushing Precinct, Dowd had the walls and bulletin boards plastered with photos of the various crime scenes. They showed the victims in their poses of death, the cars with their shattered windshields, and, most conspicuously, the many glossies of the weapon that was causing all the grief—a .44-caliber Charter Arms Bulldog revolver.

Dowd had maps of the Bronx and Queens tacked up on the walls. Each of the geographic locations of the killings and maimings was conspicuously pinpointed and identified with an appropriate marking.

In the immediate aftermath of that organized search, a decision was made—a historic first for the NYPD—to appeal personally to the .44-caliber killer.

"Son of Sam," the plea went. "We know you are not a woman hater—and know how you have suffered. We wish to help you and it is not too late. Please let us help you.

"Call Captain Borrelli or Inspector Dowd at 844-0999 or write to them at the 109th precinct, Flushing, New York."

Ten days earlier the *Daily News* had issued an appeal to the killer to surrender. It read:

The News is appealing to the killer of

Valentina Suriani and Alexander Esau to give himself up before he commits any more crimes or is killed or wounded himself. If he has any reservations about turning himself in to police or other authorities we urge him to surrender to the News. We will undertake to deliver him safely to police. If he wishes to contact the News, he may reach us at (212) 949-3648."

Neither appeal brought a response from the .44-caliber killer.

In the peripatetic trackdown of the elusive assassin it was inevitable that sooner or later they would begin preparing psychological profiles of the man committing the crimes.

One of the first to put forth his views was Dr. Harvey Schlossberg, a patrolman-turned-psychologist who, at the age of thirty-nine, was directing psychological services for the NYPD.

Schlossberg was called to conduct a study of the killer after Christine Freund's murder, just after authorities recognized that there was a pattern to the killings and maimings.

"I found this to be a very unusual case," Schlossberg said at that time. "This killer did not speak. Usually they will. They will say something, almost like a fetish, to explain why he's doing it. Or he'll take something from the victim—a ring, a piece of clothing.

"I look at everything—the style of the crime, gun, knife, does he hit the head or the stomach? The time of day it occurs, the area. And, of course, the victims. What do they have in common? In this case, the hair is obvious but I'm convinced there's something more, some connection we haven't found yet.

"Guys like this killer don't kill spontaneously. There's a sort of ritual, it's almost like choreography. It's part of the pleasure they take in building up the fantasy.

"We haven't found it yet in this case, but two, three days before a killing, he'll make a contact. Bump into the victim on the street, ask for a match. Then he spends a couple of days stalking, building up a fantasy, until it comes to the final act. It's his orgasm."

Dr. Schlossberg, who earned his Ph.D. in psychology when he wasn't doing duty as a traffic patrolman, was now in private practice in addition to his work for the Police Department. He admitted that his portrait of the killer was only a small part of the large kit of tools that the detective force was working with to track him down.

"A good detective will come up with the same kind of profile I will," Schlossberg admitted. "I can sit here with all my books and all my theories, but the detectives are sophisticated by experience. What I try to tell them is that all human behavior is perfectly understandable and even justified, according to the point of view of the person doing it, if you can just figure out what is motivating him.

What motivation or experience could turn a

person into the kind of killer who was the object of the vast manhunt?

"He is someone who is looking for help, believe it or not," Dr. Schlossberg explained. "Rather than commit suicide, he has redirected his anger toward someone else. He's lonely, he has no friends. I see him in some cheap furnished room. He's probably afraid of women. I don't know who rejected him—wife, girlfriend, sister, mother—but now his fear has turned to rage. He is very sick and really needs help."

Remember that when this saga of the .44-caliber killer has reached a climax and we are able to peek into the real suspect's psyche—remember what Dr. Schlossberg has said while the hunt was still very active and no one yet knew what the fugitive was like. And don't forget these final observations from this psychologist:

"The killer isn't stupid. Just because you're psychologically disturbed doesn't mean you're dumb. If he were simple, he would be more likely to find other ways to express his anger—taking it out physically, in athletics. But he's moody, a brooder, a thinker."

Dr. Schlossberg's last thought was that the killer's excitement had changed from the thrill of killing to the excitement of eluding the police.

"It's like poker. As the ante gets higher, the game gets more absorbing. His thing now is that we can't catch him. O.K., fine. He can fool us all he wants, but he doesn't have to keep

121

killing to taunt us. He can leave evidence, taunt us with it, but now he doesn't have to kill..."

Soon after Dr. Schlossberg had expressed those views, the voice of a noted criminal psychiatrist was heard and he was quick to label the .44-caliber killer "a classical paranoid" whose behavior pattern stood as a major stumbling block to his capture.

Dr. James Brussel had assisted the NYPD in their search for the Mad Bomber more than twenty years earlier, and the Boston police in tracking down the self-confessed Boston Strangler.

Acknowledging that the police plea to the .44-caliber killer was "an appropriate step," Brussel went on:

"They're obviously desperate and they have little to lose. But in my view, from a psychiatric perspective, it's far likelier that the man will kill again rather than turn himself in to police or even get in touch with them.

"This fellow is burning that he's got the police licked."

Brussel, who had headed the State Department of Mental Health and was now in a private practice in Greenwich Village, said he believed the killer probably held to the belief that he was godlike, above man.

"People with that kind of paranoia feel strongly that it is necessary for them to kill, and they plan their acts meticulously," Dr. Brussel said.

Referring to the note the killer left at the scene of the Suriani-Esau murders, Brussel suggested that motivation for killing might conceivably have developed after some sort of rejection, possibly under traumatic circumstances precipitated by a woman he loved.

"It is either his mother or a love interest who rejected him," Brussel suggested. "And the fact that he is attacking young women would point to the likelihood that a young woman is at the root of his problems. It is something that is burning him up.

"Everything I've seen about his description—a plain dresser who doesn't wear jewelry or other adornments—all of that points to the outward appearance of the class paranoid."

Brussel, whose views offered at that stage in the trackdown of the .44-caliber killer should also be remembered for later reference, also suggested at the time that Son of Sam "wishes to God that he is caught, but would not think of giving himself up."

The doctor held to a strong theory and which was in agreement with psychologist Schlossberg's view:

"I'd say he'll go on with another murder—or more. He doesn't take the word of man. Turning himself in would be lowering himself to manhood, and he perceives himself as being above that. He's great, but who the hell knows it?"

There they were, the psychological profiles

of the .44-caliber killer. But while profiles such as these may help give a better understanding of the kind of man the police should be looking for, the real search still had to be carried out by the guys with the gold shields, pounding the sidewalks, talking to people, snooping, searching, learning.

When Inspector Dowd finally met reporters to let them know what was going on with Task Force, he laid it on the line.

"We're going to get this guy," Dowd vowed, disdaining the use of cop jargon like "perpetrator" or "suspect."

"We'll just spend as long as it takes. There's no way we can close the file on it. I just can't wait until the end of the case. I just want to see what kind of human being this is who's been committing all these heartless killings and maimings..."

Over and above the psychological studies and profiles of the .44-caliber killer that suggested he was under demonic possession or compulsion, that he was a paranoid schizophrenic, that he was intelligent and reasonably well-educated and conceivably religious to some extent, there were other angles. The newly-shaped investigative force had begun pursuing them.

Detectives John Beccone and Richard Ward came forth with a theory that the killer may be driving a car. Although no one had seen him arrive or leave in a car, he couldn't be strictly a foot soldier. Certainly he couldn't be from the widely distant strikes he managed to make in the nine months of his terroristic reign.

Thus Beccone and Ward, with Inspector Dowd's full blessing, went off to check Motor Vehicle Bureau records of all registrations by white males, aged 20 to 30, in the past two years in Queens and the Bronx. They wanted those records to make comparisons with the .44-caliber killer's note.

But as it turned out, they couldn't have reasonably expected to make such a discovery. The MVB keeps registrations in alphabetical order. For Queens alone there were 253,000. But Detectives Beccone and Ward, fired up as they were to conduct that inquiry, simply couldn't pour through those 253,000 applications by hand.

The task force ran into other problems of a similar nature. For example, Inspector Dowd, who had an idea ahead of time that his tack wouldn't work, tried getting juvenile records to search for possible leads to the killer. But he was denied access by the courts because those records are sealed.

What Dowd was searching for was the recorded itinerary of a man, any man, who may have been arrested three years earlier or even in some more recent time in the past for molesting girls. The inspector wanted to weed out a pattern that might even remotely represent what kind of victims were being struck down now, other than the recognized similarity of long dark hair.

There were many other hinderances in

125

those early days of the Task Force search for the .44-caliber killer. But the inquiry continued relentlessly.

Then, not long afterward in late Spring, the investigation encountered a startling development. A letter with the identical slanted-hand block-lettering of the previous note left at the scene of Valerie Suriani's murder made its appearance.

It had been sent to *Daily News* columnist Jimmy Breslin.

That indeed was another major turning point in the case. But there was only one thing wrong with that gig.

Jimmy Breslin was probably the last person in the world the .44-caliber killer should have written.

CHAPTER IX

"HELLO FROM THE GUTTERS...I'M SON OF SAM"

Jimmy Breslin had been a writer with a career like a Coney Island dodgem ride, veering and bumping from one job to another on New York City newspapers.

In a shade over a half-dozen years, I recall him scootering from the *Long Island Press* to the *New York Journal-American*, to the *Herald-Tribune*. The fact that today all three newspapers are out of business should not reflect adversely on Breslin. It wasn't all his fault they folded.

In fact, Jimmy's tenure later as columnist for the *New York Post* and *Newsday*, the Long Island newspaper, had no appreciable effect on either publication's continued prosperity. Yet neither did his presence have any impact one way or another on their circulations. The papers survived and thrived despite the cherubic columnist who, in fits of convivial indelicacy, has turned author and proceated such works against the illiterately defenseless souls of organized crime as *The Gang That Couldn't Shoot Straight*.

Not long ago, the *New York Daily News*, which once upon a time haughtily bragged that its 2,225,000 daily sales were more than twice the circulation of any newspaper in America, decided in panic after plummeting paid readership to prepare against an invasion from Australia by a newspaper publishing giant named Rupert Murdoch.

In panic because by now the *News* no longer was twice as big as any other newspaper. Circulation had slipped so precipitately that the executive offices in the morning tabloid's 42nd Street skyscraper bastion buzzed with conferences.

What to do about our slipping circulation, the high command wanted to know?

Ideas were so sparse that someone suggested hiring Jimmy Breslin as a columnist. Someone else offered Pete Hamill. A third big wheel said maybe both ought to be taken on.

And thus the *News'* state of sedentariness was not solved at all since their new acquisitions, having come from opposite poles of the literary spectrum, cancelled each other out.

Prospects for improvement looked better only when the *News* became a follower—by aping the *Post's* unique, informative and gossipy *PAGE SIX* with its own *PEOPLE PAGE*, copying the afternoon daily's expanded racing, entertainment, and TV coverage, and faithfully following each innovative tactic introduced by Murdoch and his crackajack editors.

Unfortunately for the *News*, the one department in which they really wanted to outdo the *Post* they didn't succeed—in circulation gains.

While the *News'* executives were wailing to the tune of "Oh where, oh where have our 350,000 readers gone," down on South Street Murdoch's marauders were tallying up the score sheets while an ecstatic circulation director Lester Feldman couldn't believe that in a few short weeks the *Post* had picked up nearly 200,000 new readers—one of the truly remarkable circulation leaps in all of American newspaper history.

Let us now circulate to the great works of Jimmy Breslin in connection with the case of the .44-caliber killer, which is really what this chapter is all about.

Only long after the rest of the city had awakened to the menace of the .44-caliber killer did Breslin begin to hone his claws on the corpses of the victims.

That happened after Virginia Voskerichian was killed the evening of March 8th. Breslin's column about the search for her killer appeared in the *News* on March 10th. Yet there was nothing in the piece to suggest what Jimmy claimed at a much later time:

"After my column was in the paper, the ballistics people said for the first time all these shootings had been done by the same weapon, the .44."

This paragraph is excerpted from Jimmy's piece in the *News* of August 11, so perhaps his memory had faded by then about what he had written in March. The fact is that the Colossus of Queens Boulevard uttered not a sentence about any caliber of bullet in that early narrative, let alone a .44.

Adhering further to the paucity of informative reading in that previous column on the case, Breslin also made this erroneous observation:

"But the medical examiner wrote down that Virginia Voskerichian died from one shot, a large caliber lead bullet in her head. Which is the same thing that had happened to the first girl, the one who was killed on January 30."

Overlooked completely by Breslin as late as March 10th was that two other Queens girls— Joanne Lomino and Donna DeMasi—had been wounded by a mysterious gunman as long ago as November 26th, and that on the night of July 29th—eight months before that, Donna Lauria had been murdered and Jody Valente wounded by a beady-eyed assassin.

And the near fatal shooting of Carl Denaro on October 23rd in Flushing shouldn't be forgotten either.

Actually, what Breslin should have said was that his own newspaper was in truth telling the readers what Jimmy wasn't up to writing in the March 10th editions.

Reporters Thomas Pugh and William Federici had turned in notes to rewriteman Harry Stathos, who put together these revealing paragraphs which may have excaped Jimmy: "The latest victim, Virginia Voskerichian...was killed Tuesday night when an unknown assailant surprised her on a dark street near her home and shot her in the face with a .44-caliber revolver.

"Top police sources said the weapon was believed to have been the same one used to kill Christine Freund, 26, less than a block away six weeks ago, and another person in the Bronx. They suspect that all three murders may have been committed by the same person. Although homicide detectives refused to identify the murder weapon, it was reportedly an old-model .44-caliber revolver similar to ones used in the days of the old West."

Well, that only goes to show—the *News* does have some talent after all.

Yet as early as February 1st, just after Miss Freund's killing, Breslin's old paper, the *Long Island Press*, was telling its readers what Jimmy neglected to confide in his followers more than five weeks later after Miss Voskerichian's muder:

"Yesterday, the Queens medical examiner said only that the bullets were a large calibor (which killed Miss Freund). Other sources told *The Press* they were 'smashed pretty well,' making caliber determination difficult, at best.

"In the earlier incidents, a .44-caliber weapon was used."

There it is, not only did the unsigned story suggest the caliber bullet that took Miss Freund's life, but it went on to mention that the same .44-sized slugs had also felled the Misses Lomino and DeMasi and figured, too, in the Bronx case—the death of Miss Lauria and wounding of Miss Valente.

So it wasn't as Breslin said—"After my

column was in the paper, the ballistics people said for the first time all these shootings had been done by the same weapon, the .44."

We are taking time to point out all these inaccuracies and unjustified chest thumping by Breslin because we want our audience to be forewarned—Jimmy Breslin was reported writing a book on Son of Sam, the .44-caliber killer, in collaboration with Dick Schaap. The figure Viking Press is said to have advanced these "Rover Boys" is either $150,000 or $350,000, according to knowledgeable Neal Travis, editor of the *Post's PAGE SIX*.

That's some boat ride for Viking to be taken on.

Anyhow, the great emphasis on the existence of a rampaging night stalker with a deadly .44-caliber revolver wasn't made until after Mayor Beame and Commissioner Codd had called that press conference in the Flushing stationhouse and announced that the same husky-caliber Wild West-style revolver had been used in all the mysterious, unprovoked nighttime shootings.

In time, Beame, who was only doing his duty as Mayor of New York in creating the task force to track down the deadly trigger-man and keeping on top of the case, became the target of a venomous attack by Jimmy Breslin, who accused the leader of America's largest city of transforming the manhunt into a "pornographic show."

All that poor Beame had done was show up at the Flushing Precinct to check on the progress of the investigation after still another victim had been struck down by the psychopathic murderer's lethal weapon.

"Sometime back," wrote Breslin, "I made a pact with myself that I would not criticize Beame anymore. To say that he has failed the city is the same as saying that beach sand clings to ocean-wet feet. Anybody going around New York and listening in the streets and shops knows that there can be no set of circumstances under which the public will suffer the embarrassment of Beame as mayor again. Therefore I reasoned, be gentle to him at the end and recognize the fact that the man worked for the city for 40 years."

For a guy who hadn't given the city a minute of service in his whole life, Jimmy Breslin had the incredible gall to run for City Council President in the 1969 Democratic primaries. He was skunked, of course. He had fouled out with virtually every vot' · bloc— the blacks, Puerto Ricans, Jews, ...alians, Poles, Greeks, Germans. Even the Irish.

He polled 75,480 votes. More people turn out in the rain these days to watch the Cosmos play soccer.

A day came in late May when the humpbacked letter carrier from the Grand Central Post Office delivered the mail to the *Daily News* on East 42nd Street. After sorting, the newspaper's mail room delivered Jimmy Breslin's daily quota of mail to him—two letters.

One of the letters read:

"Hello from the gutters of N.Y.C. which are filled with dog manure, vomit, stale wine, urine, and blood. Hello from the sewers of N.Y.C. which swallow up these delicacies when they are washed away by the sweeper trucks. Hello from the cracks in the sidewalks of N.Y.C. and from the ants that dwell in these cracks and feed on the dried blood of the dead that has settled into the cracks.

"J.B., I'm just dropping you a line to let you know that I appreciate your interest in those recent and horrendous .44 killings. I also want to tell you that I read your column daily and find it quite informative.

"Tell me, Jim, what will you have for July Twenty-Ninth? You can forget about me if you like because I don't care for publicity. However, you must not forget Donna Lauria and you cannot let the people forget her, either. She was a very sweet girl but Sam's a thirsty lad and he won't let me stop killing until he gets his fill of blood.

"Mr. Breslin, sir, don't think that because you haven't heard from (me) for a while that I went to sleep. No, rather, I am still here. Like a spirit roaming the night. Thirsty, hungry, seldom stopping to rest; anxious to please Sam. I love my work. Now, the void has been filled.

"Perhaps we shall meet face to face someday or perhaps I will be blown away by cops with smoking .38's. Whatever, if I shall be fortunate enough to meet you I will tell you all about Sam if you like and I will introduce you to him. His name is 'Sam the Terrible.'

"Not knowing what the future holds I shall say farewell and I will see you at the next job. Or, should I say you will see my handiwork at the next job? Remember Ms. Lauria. Thank you.

"In their blood
"and
"From the Gutter.
"'Sam's Creation' .44
"P.S.: J.B., please inform all the detectives working on the slayings to remain.
"P.S.:J.B., please inform all the detectives working the case that I wish them the best of luck. 'Keep Em digging, drive on, think positive, get off your butts, knock on coffins, etc.'
"Upon my capture I promise to buy all the guys working on the case a new pair of shoes if I can get up the money.
"Son of Sam"

Directly below the bottom signature was a hand-drawn symbol, an X-shaped mark apparently intending to convey the biological signs for male and female. Above the X a cross was drawn, beneath it the initial S.

The letter was turned over to police and in one of the most incongruous ploys in journallistic annals, Jimmy Breslin wrote an appeal to the .44-caliber killer to surrender himself. But only after using every trick at his command to disenfranchise and anger the madman who'd written to him.

Here's a sample of that horrendous tact:

"The detectives, whose shoes he would buy, walk the streets at night and hope for a match with the man with the .44. 'He's mine,' one of them, a friend of mine, was saying Friday night. 'The man is Jack Ripper and I'm makin' a personal appointment with him.'"

Now follows Jimmy Breslin's personal appeal to Son of Sam, coming for the first time—indeed very deeply buried—in the thirtieth paragraph of a story that is basically an interview with Mike and Rose Lauria (J.B. didn't even know as recently as March 10th that their daughter was murdered by the .44-caliber killer):

"The hope is," said Breslin to Son of Sam finally and at last, "that the killer realizes that he is controlled by Sam, who not only forces him into acts of horror but will ultimately walk him to his death. The only way for the killer to leave this special torment is to give himself up to me, if he trusts me, or to the police, and receive both help and safety.

"If he wants any further contact, all he has to do is call or write me at *The Daily News*. It's simple to get me. The only people I don't answer are bill collectors.

"The time to do it, however, is now. We are too close to the July 29 that the killer mentions in his letter. It is the first anniversary of the death of Donna Lauria."

The *News* blew the greatest opportunity a newspaper had to end a psychopathic terrorist's stranglehold on a city since the old *Journal-American* dealt with the Mad Bomber twenty years before.

The *J-A* brought about the bomber's capture by dealing delicately and tactfully with him. They didn't tell him out of one side of their mouth that the detectives were waiting for a "match" with him, and from the other side of their mouth to surrender and receive "help and safety."

After nearly seventeen years of bombings around the city, it occurred to the newspaper's publisher, the late Seymour Berkson, to write an "Open Letter to the Mad Bomber." It was a stab in the dark, but Berkson and his editorial team believed it could pique the Bomber's interest and tempt him to bring his grievances into the open, if drafted carefully.

The letter was prepared under the direct guidance and supervision of Berkson, Managing Editor Sam H. Day, Assistant Managing Editor Paul Schoenstein, a Pulitzer Prize winner already, and City Editor Edward A. Mahar. *In collaboration* with the Police Department—a collaboration that wasn't bandied about by the *J-A* in chest-thumping fashion like a little boy saying, "Look, Mad Bomber, the cops are my buddies and they're

137

gonna wipe up the sidewalk with you, so better give up ..." No, not the Jimmy Breslin leaded glove approach at all.

The Mad Bomber hadn't even written to the *Journal-American*. Berkson and his team felt the proper approach might just bring a response and tip off his identity to police.

Here's how the first letter was framed on Page 1 in all editions of December 26, 1956:

"Give yourself up.

"For your own welfare and for that of the community, the time has come for you to reveal your identity.

"The *N. Y. Journal-American* guarantees that you will be protected from any illegal action and that you will get a fair trial.

"This newspaper also is willing to help you in two other ways.

"It will publish all the essential parts of your story as you may choose to make it public.

"It will give you the full chance to air whatever grievances you may have as the motive for your acts.

"We urge you to accept this offer now not only for your own sake but for the sake of the community.

"Time is running out on your prospects of remaining unapprehended.

"You can telephone the City Editor of this newspaper at COrtlandt 7-1212, or you can go to any police station or even the policeman on the street and tell him who you are.

"In all cases you will be given the benefits of our American system of justice.

"Give yourself up now."

Writing and editing such a letter to a then nameless and faceless person was no simple task. Several drafts were revised before the final one was agreed upon. Every indication of the bomber's mentality and motivation was studied and each word chosen to win his confidence.

The letter asked him to surrender but it offered him the chance to do so with dignity and guarantees that he would not be harmed; it offered opportunity to air whatever grievances he had that motivated his acts—and assured fair and just treatment.

Two days after the letter was published, a copy boy brought Assistant City Editor Richard Piperno an envelope addressed to the newspaper in distinctive hand-blocked lettering. Piperno's intuition told him the letter just might be from the Mad Bomber. So he put on a pair of light gloves and cut the envelope open with a scissor.

Then he extracted the letter inside with a tweezer, opened it, saw it indeed was a response to the *J-A's* appeal.

But was the letter from the Mad Bomber himself—or from a prankster or crank?

That wasn't Piperno's decision to make. In

accordance with arrangements the publisher and editors had made with Police Commissioner Stephen P. Kennedy, the letter was delivered to headquarters and turned over to the police laboratory.

But not a word of that routine was mentioned in the news stories. The writer pledged a "truce" in his bombing activities until mid-January. He listed places where he had placed explosives in 1956 (for police purposes this amounted to a written confession). He provided fragments of new information about himself, revealing "my days on earth are numbered."

The bomber indicated his grievances originated when he was injured while working for the Consolidated Edison Company and failed to receive what he considered fair or adequate compensation for his injuries. Con Ed is the utility which periodically plunges New York City into darkness.

The *Journal-American* had won its first victory. It had obtained a temporary halt in the terror bombing. The primary goal of the "Open Letter" had been public safety.

After the secretive investigation for clues at the lab was completed, the *J-A* published the bomber's letter and ran another appeal—asking for more information about his grievance with the utility company. The bomber responded; again his letter was published and still another plea for more information was inserted on Page 1.

The bomber answered once more and by

now enough information had been divulged by the writer that detectives were able to trace the file of a disgruntled former employee at Con Ed to his lair. The rest was routine as the story in the *J-A* of January 22, 1957 reads:

"Acting on information supplied by the *N. Y. Journal-American*, police last night captured the Mad Bomber in Waterbury, Conn.

"He is George Metesky, 53, a mild-mannered, sickly bachelor who lived with two spinster sisters in a ramshackle gray frame house at 17 Fourth St.—in the Brooklyn section of Waterbury.

"His capture and confession ended one of the greatest police manhunts in New York's history.

"It was through this newspaper's three-week long unprecedented exchange of written communications with the Mad Bomber that the man who eluded police dragnets for 16 years was finally apprehended..."

I'm very proud of that story because I wrote it. I was a member of the *J-A* team that shaped the appeals to the Mad Bomber. I also wrote all the banner headline stories through that period and those that followed his arrest that resulted in his confinement for sixteen years in a state hospital for the criminal insane, after which he was released as cured.

I shared in seventeen journalistic awards with the publisher and editors of the *Journal-*

141

American in recognition of the way we helped bring about an end to the Mad Bomber's reign.

Editorials in newspapers around the world lauded our form of responsible journalism, but I believe the way the *New York Times* put it tells it best for purposes of this story on Son of Sam, the .44-caliber killer:

"One has to hunt for a lesson to be drawn from all this travail. But it may be found in the fact that what finally led to a solution of this particular police case was an appeal based on sympathy... This appeal was made by the *N. Y. Journal-American*, and it struck a note that brought the response from a sick mind waiting for just such a chance to pour out his grievances."

Nobody, but nobody could ever say that about the roles Jimmy Breslin and the *Daily News* played in the Son of Sam case.

CHAPTER X

OUTSIDE A JUMPIN' DISCO

It was 3:20 o'clock on the Sunday morning of June 26th.

Exactly seventy days almost to the hour since the .44-caliber killer last struck, which was in the Bronx when he claimed Valentina Suriani and Alexander Esau as the fourth and fifth fatalities on his grim scorecard, totaling nine victims when counting the four wounded.

Fear that this madman would murder again had not abated anywhere. Especially not since his recent note indicated quite plainly that he wasn't about to let up:

"I will see you at the next job. Or, should I say you will see my handiwork at the next job?"

When seventeen-year-old Judy Placido and twenty-year-old Sal Lupo got into the front seat of a borrowed car that Sunday morning at the curb in front of a one-family house at 45-39 211th Street in Bayside, Queens, they shared a cigarette and a great deal of conversation about the .44-caliber killer.

That was all they had heard all night long in the Elephas discotheque around the corner on Northern Boulevard.

Judy herself, who had graduated earlier Saturday from St. Catherine's Academy in the Bronx—the school Valentina Suriani once attended—was uptight about Son of Sam.

Her fright was grounded in the knowledge that the .44-caliber killer had struck, both the first time, then the last time out, in her very own neighborhood. Judy lived at 2208 Wickham Avenue, alongside the grounds of Bronx State Hospital, a mental institution.

Even early on Saturday before Judy joined some friends who drove over the Whitestone Bridge to Queens to celebrate, there'd been talk about the two neighborhood killings.

Judy's sister, Donna, who was twenty-four and lived in Ohio, had flown to the city Friday night for the graduation which was held in Cardinal Spellman High School on the Grand Concourse. Out in Ohio they had run stories about the .44-caliber killer but the newspapers didn't give too many details since Son of Sam wasn't as much of a menace there as the National Guard was to the people of the Buckeye State. So Donna asked a lot of questions about the two attacks in the neighborhood which had taken three lives and wounded one. And Judy brought Donna up to date.

All Friday night and again Saturday morning as it began to rain, Donna discussed the .44-caliber killer with her sister and members of their family. Donna couldn't get the killer out of her mind and she warned Judy repeatedly to be very careful and avoid sitting in parked cars—but especially about wearing her long brown hair down.

"Okay, Donna," Judy said surrenderingly after Saturday night dinner at the neat and well-cared-for home where Judy who, since her mother's death eight years before, had lived with her aunt and legal guardian, Judith Carioscia. "I'll wear my hair up if it makes you happy."

The conversation wasn't all about the .44-caliber killer. Some of the talk at the buffet party dwelled on Judy's future—her plans to attend Pace University's College of White Plains in the Fall on a partial scholarship.

Yes, Judy had brains, a good head on her shoulders. Her long-range goal was to be a lawyer.

After the food began to run out and the repartee turned to other topics, Judy let it be known that it was time for her to go. And with the typical vivaciousness and drive of the buoyant, fun-loving teenager which Judy Placido was, she said her goodbyes to Aunt Judith, to Donna, to brother John, and his wife, Cathy, all of whom had come to celebrate the big day.

Then at 11 p.m. Judy, still wearing her white graduation gown, was off with her three girlfriends for a night on the town.

"Let's go to the Elephas," somebody said as the car crossed into Queens. The suggestion met with unanimous approval because the Elephas was one of the most popular disco-teques in that borough.

Although situated on busy Northern Boulevard, one of Queens' most heavily-traveled thoroughfares, the Elephas also was, incongruously, adjacent to a quiet residential neighborhood where middle-class families had not been able to adjust to the noisy weekend nights. The blare of hard rock music deafened ears and the invasion of cars and young people transformed the area into a carnival atmosphere that was pandemic for blocks around.

But on that Saturday night the crowds had been slow in arriving because rainstorms had plagued the city. Later on, however, as the rains let up, the crowds swarmed into the Elephas.

Her evening at the dimly-lighted disco was glorious for Judy—and, as always, it was glorious for the girl-watchers, too. For when Judy Placido danced she was stunning and quite devastating. Always fashionably tailored, the fun-loving Judy could whirl like a ballerina on the crowded dance floor and seem as though she were the only one doing the number.

Judy's beauty wasn't in evidence only at discos. Just that recent past Winter she'd been elected Snow Princess of the Snow Queen dance at St. Catherine's.

On that Saturday night, Judy was in a particularly happy mood for there'd been the achievement of graduation to give her that added headiness. But then for a brief while at the Elephas Judy felt suddenly disturbed. A young man with black hair and gray shirt began to hassle her and Judy was put out. She left the round dance floor and went to the bar where Sal Lupo was nursing a Scotch and waiting to do a turn with Judy to the music that the disco's disk jockey, Tony C, was piping from the glittery booth at the edge of the dance floor.

Judy had known Sal for some months now, having met him and danced with him at the Elephas. On more than a few occasions since, Judy and Sal bumped into each other at the disco. But they never really dated. They got along well, however, and it was never more obvious than that Saturday night when Judy ambled over to Sal and complained about the dude who'd gotten on her back.

Sal knew that guys were always giving girls a rough time in discos, so he played it cool. He turned for a brief moment, sized up the character from the back, didn't think he recognized him, then smiled at Judy and said, "Cool it, okay? He's out of it."

Sal had arrived at the Elephas a while after Judy and her friends. He had driven there with his buddy, Ralph, as he often had done, and they parked in front of a house with a white picket fence on 211th Street, a block south from Northern Boulevard.

They walked to the Elephas and each of them plunked down a five dollar bill for two tickets that were their price of admission and good for two drinks apiece.

Sal, the sixth of seven sons of a father named Salvatore, lived in Maspeth, had gone to Grover Cleveland High School in Ridgewood, and worked now and then at a gas station in Glendale that was managed by his brother John. Sal had many friends, including the disco's bouncer, Ralph Sacenti, who owned a 1972 maroon Cadillac Coupe de Ville.

"Hey, Ralph, baby," Lupo nudged the bulky bouncer a few minutes after 3 o'clock that Sunday morning. "Think I can use your car to take Judy home?"

"No sweat, Sal," replied Sacenti, digging into his pocket and handing the ignition key to his friend.

"Only I'll do the driving, Sal," the bouncer sneered good naturedly. "Here are the keys, good buddy. Go out and wait for me."

"Right on," Lupo smiled. Then he wheeled and went to take Judy by the arm. He was escorting her home because Judy's friends, terrified about the .44-caliber killer, had left earlier. She had assured them that Sal would get her home one way or another.

Judy and Sal strolled out of the Elephas and went down 211th Street where Sacenti had told Lupo the Caddy was parked. It was under a huge, overgrown twenty-nine-year-old maple on the lawn in front of the house at 45-39 211th Street. The tree had been planted as a sapling by the developer in 1948.

The car was locked. Lupo opened the door and flicked the other door lock so Judy could get in from the passenger side next to the sidewalk.

"How about a cigarette?" were Judy's first words.

"You got it," Sal replied, taking a pack from his pocket and pulling out a cigarette.

But he couldn't find a match and decided to light up with the car's cigarette lighter. But the car was strange to him. So he foundered around a while and found the light switch on the dashboard. In that instant that the lights inside the car were on, Sal managed to light the cigarette, puff out its smoke, and put the cigarette between Judy's lips.

Then with one hand he shut off the lights and the other went around Judy's shoulder.

"So what's new about the .44-caliber killer?" Lupo asked almost as though he didn't believe there could be a threat from the killer on the block they were parked.

Judy, in fact, couldn't have been much concerned either for she had let her long hair down while dancing and had not bothered to take it up as she had promised at home.

"All night at my house, that's all we talked about," Judy said. "Even here in the disco everyone's worried about him ..."

They were in the car barely ten minutes. Then all at once it happened—just as in six previous times. A flash of light and a terrifying explosion, followed by another, then another, and finally a fourth one. All in rapid succession.

Judy screamed in pain. Sal winced as he felt the excruciating sting of something harsh and cold on his right arm, the one he had around Judy.

"Some crazy sonofabitch shot at us," Lupo cried as he wrangled himself out of the front seat.

"Hey, Judy," he shouted, "I'm going to get help..."

He had felt the blood on Judy's head and knew she couldn't be moved. He ran up the block, back to the Elephas and bumped into Ralph Sacenti at the door.

"I'm shot...Judy's hit bad..." Lupo wailed. "Did you hear the shots?"

Back at the car, just after Lupo ran to summon help, Judy Placido had managed to open the door on her side and stumbled out.

She staggered for about twenty feet in the middle of the roadway on 211th Street. Then she crumpled to the blacktop some fifteen feet from 45th Road.

That was where bouncer Sacenti, Lupo, and the others from the Elephas found her when they ran out to size up Judy's condition.

Meanwhile, a resident of 211th Street who heard the shots and persons inside the Elephas who'd been alerted to the gunfire and Judy's injury phoned police.

Detective Sergeant Edward Danlem was one of the first sleuths on the scene, responding from the nearest precinct, the 111th, which was a mere three blocks away at 40-30 214th Place in Bayside.

This was the same stationhouse that an unidentified male had phoned the previous week and said, "This is Son of Sam. Next week I'm going to hit Bayside."

The message was passed on to the Task Force but, like so many other threats and information that was pouring in, this
150

message received only routine attention.

But the watch by Task Force was conducted on the systematic basis that had been mandated by Inspector Dowd and the others who were conducting the search for Son of Sam. Thus the Elephas was under surveillance. Or, at least, a team had been directed to stake out the place—just in case.

The ambulance arrived and Miss Placido and Lupo were taken to Flushing Hospital. Lupo, a walking wounded, was put into a wheelchair. Doctors had quickly decided the scoring on his right arm and leg would need surgery—but Judy Placido had to be tended to immediately because her condition was critical.

She'd been struck by three bullets, all in dangerous areas of the upper body and head. One had entered behind the right ear, a second went into the neck and lodged perilously close to the spinal cord, and the the third bored into her right shoulder.

As surgeons ministered to the patients, Judy's and Sam's alarmed families gathered in the fourth floor waiting room. They'd never met before, but now they were united by a common link—tragedy wrought by the phantom assassin whose bullets had felled these two young people as his tenth and eleventh victims.

Judy was still in surgery now and her aunt, Mrs. Carioscia, looked at her watch and shook her head.

"I wonder how much longer?" she asked.

151

"Don't worry," said Donna, "Judy is strong. She will pull out of it all right..."

Then Donna shook her head.

"I knew it...I knew it...I felt it inside me, a premonition. I didn't want Judy to go out tonight..."

Now a man in a green hospital gown appeared down the hall. The doctor who performed the surgery on Judy. He had a report for the family. Judy had come through the operation in fine shape.

"She'll make it," he smiled.

That same doctor had also removed three bullets from Judy and as tests would soon show, they were .44-caliber slugs and had been fired from the same Charter Bulldog that had killed and wounded nine other persons before that morning.

In the entire United States only 28,000 models of this weapon had been sold, a piddling number in contrast to the millions of guns that pass over the counters each year. Yet only one out of all those 28,000 was the gun that Inspector Dowd and his Task Force were trying to trace.

For a brief, blinding instant it had been brought out of hiding as the madman behind its trigger cut another swath upon the landscape and then just as quickly disappeared.

Now as on those rare occasions past, police again had eyewitnesses. There were two. Both pedestrians and both with identical reports to police. They had seen a man, about 5 feet 10 and 170 pounds fleeing the scene of the shooting. He was wearing a beige three-quarter length coat and—for the first time—was seen driving away in a car, a mustard colored sedan!

"We not only have witnesses who observed him running away but who have provided us with a solid description," said a triumphant Inspector Dowd.

"Now, too, we've learned a little more about the way he operates, the way he selected his victims..."

None of the witnesses had seen him fire at Judy and Sam. And as Detective Sergeant Richard Conlan would soon report to his boss, neither had the victims seen the gunman.

"Lupo says he only saw the blinding flash of the gun," Conlan said. "Judy saw nothing...she just felt the bullets hitting her and pain..."

Someone began counting wounds. For the first time now the .44-caliber killer had inflicted the largest number of wounds on a single outing. Five. Did that mean Son of Sam was getting so bold that he was no longer saving the last bullet for his brain in case the police threatened to capture him?

No, not that. He still had fired only four bullets. The bullet that went through Lupo's arm was the same one that clipped his leg.

Lupo was also questioned at length about the young man Judy had pointed out as her annoyer on the dance floor. But detectives soon checked him and found he had the perfect alibi. He had remained in the discotheque after Judy and Sam went to the car.

Of all the detectives working on the case—now Task Force had been swelled to fifty men and women searchers—none was as disappointed as Timothy Dowd about the unfortunate turn of events that early Sunday morning, a turn that could have gotten the police their man.

"The case could easily have ended outside the Elephas," bemoaned Dowd. "But one of our teams that had the place staked out was called on a tip to another locale a few minutes earlier."

Dowd said that even with no detail on the spot when the shooting occurred, the police response was immediate.

"We've created a tactical system that can respond to a situation like this instantly," he explained. "And in a sense the system worked well. We were there within two minutes after the call came in..."

But that still wasn't quick enough. The .44-caliber killer had struck again and again he had outfoxed the hunters.

Son of Sam was still as free as the wind. Or, as Commissioner Codd commented after the latest shootings:

"This is worse than looking for a needle in a haystack. In that situation at least you know where the haystack is. Here we don't even know what the haystack looks like..."

CHAPTER XI

STEPPING UP THE MANHUNT

It was more than just a manhunt by fifty detectives.

The search for Son of Sam, the .44-caliber killer had been mounted by an entire city. There were the rest of the members of the NYPD, patrolmen, detectives, sergeants, lieutenants, and on up in every precinct in the city. Theoretically they were searching for the phantom marauder every waking hour.

The Task Force also had in its ranks working for it such varied experts as astrologers, psychiatrists, psychologists, sociologists, parole officers, and just about any person with any investigatory or deductive acumen in the mammoth search for the crazed killer.

The composite sketches were appearing in the daily press more often. Calls were pouring into the 109th Precinct's command post with information, particularly tips of potential suspects whose looks resembled the drawings.

Yet the flood of calls didn't titillate Detective Sergeant Edward Dahlem, as one of the officers in charge of sorting through the daily pile of Task Force assignment sheets on which each "clue" offered by an incoming call was jotted down.

"Everyone knows someone who looks good,

someone who looks like the composite," Dahlem complained. "The problem is that there have been different composites since last March. But we've got to check out each lead, each clue. I'd hate to be the one who let the right one pass by me."

A detective twenty years, Dahlem called out the names of Detectives Frank Pergola and Gerald Shevlin. Meanwhile the phones were jangling something fierce.

"Yes, yes...slow down, please slow down...I've got to write this," a detective was barking into one mouthpiece. "You saw a man who looks like Son of Sam looking into parked cars...Okay, give me the location, please..."

Another detective was on the horn with a detective in another precinct. He was pleading, "All I ask you is please check the guy out...somebody made a strong case for the killer...You will, okay thanks a bunch..."

Pergola and Shevlin had arrived at Sergeant Dahlem's desk. He handed the sheaf of assignment sheets to Shevlin.

"You've got four to check out there. They look pretty good, so make the most of it."

Since March 8th, after Virginia Voskerichian had been murdered and Task Force was formed, Pergola and Shevlin had chased after more than three hundred leads—leads that resulted in eliminating three hundred suspects.

That was the kind of trackdown of the phantom assassin the NYPD was conducting. It was all out. And it wasn't just out of the

109th that the biggest effort was being expended.

Some of the most productive work in the long-running investigation was being performed in a cluttered, eighth-floor office that was the Police Ballistics Section at 235 East 20th Street in Manhattan.

It was in this testing ground that the NYPD's ballistics sleuths first determined that the slug removed from Donna Lauria's body and the other lead missile that had wounded Jody Valente had been triggered from a .44-caliber Bulldog revolver manufactured by Charter Arms.

The bullets taken from the killer's first job and all the others along the way, which thus far had left five dead and six maimed, had all been brought to this laboratory. Each of the bullets was placed in a brown envelope and delivered downtown and put through the rigid testing and examination required to determine the identity of the missile.

Once those first bullets from the Bronx were identified as .44s, they were compared—their rifling marks are like fingerprints at the scene of a crime—with other .44-caliber bullets in the open file. The open file contains slugs fired by weapons known and unknown, recovered and not recovered from other cases.

Of course those bullets didn't compare to any. That meant the slugs which killed Donna and wounded Jody were fired by a .44 Charter Arms Bulldog without a previous history of use in any New York area crime.

The man who ran that ballistics scientific team was Captain James Horan, a twenty-year veteran of the department with two master's degrees. Under his direction in the lab were some of the best firearms experts in the world.

They were handling more than 17,000 cases a year—every gun, every bullet in any criminal case anywhere in the five boroughs of the city had to end up in their lab for analysis.

At that point in time, their search was concentrated as perhaps never before for clues and evidence on .44-caliber revolvers. Whenever a .44 Bulldog was found by a cop anywhere in the city, he'd ship it immediately to the lab for inspection and tests.

The testing consisted of firing a bullet into a large tank of water; the bullet loses momentum in the liquid and settles to the bottom.

A long stick with putty on the end of it is poked into the water and encased around the slug—that is done so the markings won't be altered or obliterated. The bullet is pulled out of the tank and placed under a ballistics microscope.

The instrument actually has the effect of being a twin microscope. The dual lenses are bridged optically and a binocular eyepiece enables the viewer to examine the bullet fired from the suspect gun, as well as the one used to kill or injure by the .44-caliber killer. The trick is to line up the markings on the two slugs by turning each one until the rifling marks match up.

At that point of time—in the aftermath of the Judy Placido-Sam Lupo attack in Queens, ballistics had already examined scores of guns; they were test fired and matchups were attempted. But disappointingly, there'd been no matchups so far.

In their unrelenting effort to get a bead on the madman, police touched up their anatomical portrait of the killer and came up with the following characteristics:

• He was polite, college-educated, white, pale-faced, clear-skinned.

• Days he worked at some kind of paperwork—perhaps as a clerk or a writer. He was good at it.

• Nights he was a loner, almost certainly not married.

• He had few friends—almost certainly no women friends or a lover.

• Some nights his sexual frustration and schizophrenic anguish erupted so turbulantly that he stalked another victim—another young woman with long brown hair.

• His murderous rampages may be instigated by a great trauma he suffered. As Inspector Timothy Dowd put it, "That could have been the loss of a loved one or a reflect to jilting by a potential female partner. He apparently doesn't know how to meet and treat and conduct affairs with women; he cannot establish a good relationship with a young woman."

- He lead a lonely life. If he lived in a family situation he probably had his own room.
- Quite intelligent. Very bright. Very cunning.
- His religious references in two letters indicated he was Catholic or Episcopalian.

By July 2nd, Police Commissioner Codd, trying to avoid another Elephas episode on a weekend ordered an additional two dozen radio patrol cars into Queens and Bronx neighborhoods in a beefed-up security dragnet to thwart a possible new strike by the .44-caliber maniac. The patrol now totalled fifty-six unmarked cars in the two boroughs.

Meanwhile, Chief of Detectives Keenan directed the mailing of more than 2000 letters to state, city and federal law enforcement agencies, banks, and private security firms in the Metropolitan Area asking for the names of employees licensed to carry a .44.

Now came another plea to the .44-caliber killer to surrender. It was from Inspector Dowd:

"Please get in touch with me. You're not solving your problems. We'll give you all the help we can. We know that you are suffering pain and anguish and we understand that you are not in control of yourself.

"You must make that supreme effort to communicate with us, or anyone. We will do what we can to alleviate your problems."

Then *Daily News* columnist Pete Hamill got into the act undoubtedly motivated by the belief that Son of Sam might understand the English Pete writes better than Jimmy Breslin's:

"All right, you made your points. You have shown that you can still come out of the darkness with your .44-caliber Bulldog revolver, and kill or maim the innocent, despite the largest manhunt in this city's recent history. You have mocked the police and shot two more human beings, and lived to read your own reviews. You have forced yourself up out of the dark corners of this city's imagination, and now you people the dreams of thousands. You have proved, above all, that you exist.

"But there is nothing left now to prove. You cannot kill every young woman with long, dark hair. You cannot even kill everyone parked in cars late at night. You are faced now with the implacable logic of sheer numbers; there will always be more people than you can kill.

"So now is the time to end your desperate season. You can do it very easily. You can walk into this newspaper and surrender. If you are afraid of the police, we will go with you through every step of the process. Or you can call the homicide cops directly. They will meet you anywhere. They will not kill you. Cops see too much pain, grief and blood in the ordinary course of their days to want to add to the total. They just want the killing to stop..."

Needless to say, the Son of Sam, the .44-caliber killer didn't heed Inspector Dowd's impassioned plea nor Hamill's eloquent call to reason.

The man with the big cannon was still free to strike again...

CHAPTER XII

A COMPLAINT IN YONKERS

On April 10th, Sam Carr had received a letter at his home, 316 Warburton Avenue in Yonkers. He opened it and read:

"This is to inform you that I'm in the process of filing legal papers in Yonkers City Court to have one of your dogs removed from our property cause he is a public nuisance.

"... Our lives have been torn apart because of this dog..."

The writer, who signed the letter Anonymous, asked the 64-year-old retired City of Yonkers employee to rid himself of his black Labrador retriever, Harvey, a trained guard dog.

Carr called to his wife, Frances, who conducted a telephone answering service at the house. He also summoned two of their three grown children who lived with the parents, twenty-six-year-old daughter Wheat and twenty-four-year-old Michael. Their eldest son, John, 30, lived in North Dakota.

"Who in creation would write this letter?" Carr asked his family. No one could advance an answer.

"Well," shrugged Carr, "probably some crank...maybe a nut. Let's forget about it."

Ten days went by and Carr had all but

forgotten the letter threatening court action over the dog. But the writer hadn't let the complaint rest there. He was at it again with another missive, written as the first one in black ink and long hand. It read:

"Samuel Carr,

"I have asked you kindly to stop that dog from howling all day long, yet he continues to do so. I pleaded with you. I told you how it is destroying my family—we have no peace, no rest.

"Now I know what kind of person you are, and what kind of family you are. You are cruel and inconsiderate. You have no love for any other human beings. Your (sic) selfish, Mr. Carr.

"My life is destroyed now. I have nothing to lose anymore. I can see that there shall be no peace in my life or my families(sic) life until I end yours.

"You wicked evil man—child of the devil. I curse you and your family forever. I pray to God that he takes your whole family off the face of this earth. People like you should not be allowed to live on this planet.

"A Citizen"

The thin, grey-haired Carr was now beside himself.

Who could this neighbor be, he asked? Over and over he posed the same question to himself, to his family. But no one had even the foggiest notion.

Seven more days went by but the anonymous letter-writer had not been forgotten by Carr this time. He had wondered on a few occasions about the merits of showing the letters to the Yonkers police. But he decided against it. Who knows, he said to himself, maybe this letter will be the last time I hear from that weirdo.

It was now 9:30 a.m. of April 27th. All at once Carr was jarred by a loud explosion in the back yard, followed immediately by the plaintive yelping of his dog.

Carr bolted to the window and looked out just in time to catch sight of a huskily-built man of medium height in blue jeans and a yellow-red shirt running north along the aqueduct which is also alongside the seven-story apartment house whose back faces Sam Carr's yard and fronts on Pine Street.

As the fleeing man disappeared behind a clutch of shrubs, Carr's attention was instantly drawn by Harvey, whose whining had continued uninterruptedly. From what Carr noticed now, the dog apparently had been injured. He was limping, then squatting and trying to lick at its right hind leg.

Carr went to the back yard and sure enough Harvey had been hurt. Blood was trickling from the leg.

As Carr would soon find out, Harvey had been shot and the bullet had lodged deep into the dog's thigh.

Now he could no longer put up with the

phantom who hated his dog. Carr phoned the Yonkers police and Officers Peter Intervallo and Thomas Chamberlain came to the house.

This wasn't the first time that Carr had an encounter with Yonkers police on a complaint. The previous October someone started a fire that burned the Carrs' front door, but no, the arsonist was never found nor was any motive for the act pinpointed.

Carr showed the detectives the two letters and told about that morning's episode in the back yard.

Intervallo and Chamberlain wrote down all the information and promised Carr they'd investigate. They also took the letters with them for study.

A psychiatrist was asked by the police to give an opinion about the person who wrote them.

"Definitely a schizophrenic..." was his conclusion.

But that's where it all ended for the time being. The police didn't pick up the letter-writer's trail then, nor that of the man who apparently pegged the shot at Sam Carr's dog. There was no question in the minds of police or of Carr that the person who wounded Harvey had also sent the letters. However, finding him was like looking for the haystack which Commissioner Codd had spoken about.

Seven weeks passed. It was June 14th now and suddenly the Yonkers police had cause to rekindle the probe of the anonymous letter-writer and the wounding of Carr's Labrador retriever.

Jack Cassara, a resident of New Rochelle, another Westchester County city, had generated the renewed interest in Carr's experience with the phantom letter-writer. Cassara had received a weird condolence card.

The text of the anonymous note, which had the picture of a dog on the front side, read:

"Dear Jack,

"Sorry to hear you fell off the roof. Please be more careful next time.

"P.S. Since you'll be laid up for some time, maybe Nann will need help."

It was signed "Mr. and Mrs. Samuel Carr."

Neither Cassara nor his wife Nann knew any folks named Carr. They also weren't in the mood for nonsense like that. They were preparing for the funeral of Cassara's uncle, Catrenze Cassara, who had died two days earlier at the age of ninety-two.

But a note like that couldn't be overlooked, especially since it was signed by apparently legitimate people. So Mrs. Cassara, prepared to give a piece of her mind, looked up the Carr's phone number and dialed it. She spoke to Mrs. Carr.

Absolutely not her doing, nor anyone else's in her family, she assured Mrs. Cassara. But, hold on a moment!

Mrs. Carr had an idea who that idiot writer might be—the same jerk who sent her husband the two warning notes about the dog and who also shot Harvey in the leg.

By now the wounding of their dog was even more painful, for it had cost the Carrs more than $1000 for treatments at the veterinarian's. But worse, the large-caliber slug was still in the dog's thigh and could not be removed. If it were, Harvey'd be crippled.

Mrs. Carr told Mrs. Cassara that the Yonkers police were investigating her case and suggested the Cassaras show their crazy postcard to New Rochelle Police.

Cassara, who worked at the Neptune Worldwide Moving Company in New Rochelle, took the note to police. But unlike Sam Carr, who couldn't imagine what nut would climb on his spine like that, Jack Cassara had an opinion who sent that bizarre greeting.

"I know the world has got a lot of nuts running around," he told New Rochelle detectives. He cited the episode at Neptune the past February 14th when a warehouseman who worked with Cassara went berserk, took hostages, and killed six of them in the plant.

But what did that mass killing have to do with the condolence note that Cassara received? Well, just that Cassara had his suspicions about the mentality and stability of another person he knew.

Who was that, the police asked?

The man in mind was a David Berkowitz who once had rented a room from Cassara.

But why would Berkowitz write such a card to Cassara?

Because Berkowitz was a disgruntled lodger in Cassara's house. He left in a huff and he could very well be taking it out on his former landlord now with this bizarre retaliation.

That information didn't go unheeded, although the New Rochelle police themselves did not seek out Berkowitz for investigation. They found that David Richard Berkowitz, a 24-year-old ex-soldier and presently a postal worker in the Bronx, didn't reside in their jurisdiction.

He lived at 35 Pine Street, on the top or seventh floor—the same building that backs against Sam Carr's yard!

When the information from New Rochelle made its way to Yonkers police, it was turned over to Detectives Intervallo and Chamberlain who at once took a deep interest in David Berkowitz, if for no other reason than his geographical proximity to the much-maligned Sam Carr.

Intervallo and Chamberlain first went and spoke with Cassara. Berkowitz was a lodger for three months in early 1974 in a second-floor room of the Cassaras' two-story house at 172 Coligni Street.

Cassara couldn't put his finger on any specific thing but it was Berkowitz's general "weirdness" that prompted him to point a finger at him.

"I can't think of anyone else who would do

such a thing," Cassara said.

Well, the detectives had to start somewhere. So they zeroed in on David Berkowitz, who they learned had lived at No. 35 Pine since he moved from New Rochelle in April of 1976.

They did not go near the suspect but they worked all around him.

They found, for example, that some neighbors regarded Berkowitz as a loner and eccentric. Those labels in themselves didn't make the young man an author of threatening and depraved notes or a menace who shoots dogs.

Yet the sleuths also learned that shortly after he had moved in he ran downstairs shouting, "I don't like dogs barking."

Intervallo and Chamberlain came up with more interesting findings when they checked his address before New Rochelle. They learned from superintendent James Lynch that David Berkowitz's year-long stay had been a most disturbing one.

For one thing, an 84-year-old woman living on the floor below him had received a threatening note accompanied by demands to turn down the volume of her TV set.

The woman happened to have been hard of hearing. The notes upset her but she didn't complain to police. She was afraid they'd arrest her.

So what she did was lower the volume and sit closer to the set so she could hear the sound.

There'd also been an incident with a dog there.

The dog belonging to the children of the superintendent of the building next door had been killed by a shot fired from a window in the apartment house where Berkowitz lived. The dog was buried in a lot behind the house.

What was that which the Son of Sam had written to Captain Borrelli...?"

"When father Sam gets drunk he gets mean. He beats his family. Sometimes he ties me up to the back of the house. Other times he locks me in the garage. Sam loves to drink blood."

Then...

"Behind our house some rest. Mostly young—raped and slaughtered—their blood drained—just bones now..."

Was he referring to the superintendent's children's dog in that last paragraph?

Or to Sam Carr's Labrador retriever in the earlier paragraph that he might have believed he had killed?

Whatever the reference, how could Detectives Intervallo and Chamberlain ever be expected to make that connection between the Yonkers episodes and the striking references in that note to Captain Borrelli?

The Westchester detectives were not actively involved nor had they ever been associated with any phase connected with the .44-caliber killer's case.

But then all of a sudden they were involved. Tangentially, yet involved.

Because they picked up so many disturbing soundings about David Berkowitz, Intervallo and Chamberlain speculated, even suspected, that the guy in the $265-a-month one-bedroom apartment on the seventh floor of No. 35 Pine—well, maybe, just maybe...

When the detectives went to their supervisor, Sergeant Mike Nobotny with those thoughts, he didn't think they were so wild.

"No, I don't think you guys are off the wall at all," Nobotny assured them. "In fact, I have an idea. Upstairs right at this moment is one of the elite detectives from the NYPD. He's here tracking down some leads in the Son of Sam case. Go and bounce your idea on him."

Detective Richard Salverson of the Intelligence Division had come to Yonkers to follow up a suggestion the cops check out such places as Yonkers and New Rochelle and Mount Vernon, all within a few minutes' driving and commuting distance from the Bronx, where the night stalker had struck three out of seven times.

And because of parkway links with Queens, the killer could also find getting to the scene of his other five murderous assaults hardly any more difficult than getting to the Bronx targets.

Of course the alienists also had suggested the same kind of study and search be made in Nassau County, which borders on Queens.

Salverson closeted himself with Intervallo and Chamberlain and let them offer their data on the suspect.

The Yonkers sleuths recall him telling them:

"It sounds good. You've got more than

anybody downtown has..."

But David Berkowitz was not approached for questioning. He wasn't even placed under surveillance by the Task Force.

The information from Detectives Intervallo and Chamberlain was mere suspicion based on hunches and upon inferences drawn from other inferences.

They weren't able to tie David Berkowitz to the notes sent Sam Carr and Jack Cassara. Nor could they come even remotely close to pinning the shooting of Carr's dog on him.

With so many other angles to chase after, should the NYPD waste time and manpower on an oddball in Yonkers? Let the cops in the sticks worry about him...

CHAPTER XIII

ANNIVERSARY OF FEAR

Not the police, not anyone wanted it to happen. But it did. The first anniversary of the .44-caliber killer had arrived and his identity and whereabouts were as perplexing as the moment he first struck in the Bronx 365 long, tortured days ago.

The most dangerous, most elusive criminal ever to roam the streets of New York City continued to evade the largest dragnet ever assembled to stalk that killer who called himself Son of Sam.

Long before the milestone date of July 29, 1977, people began playing guessing games—generated by saturation newspaper coverage—about the man with the deadly cannon.

Would that monster with a thirst for pretty young women with long, dark hair mark his first year of terror with another bloody assault?

If he did, what ground would he desecrate next? Would it be the Bronx or Queens again, his chosen territories so far for spreading his uniquely gruesome brand of terror?

"Tell me, Jim, what will you have for July 29?" the killer had written to Jimmy Breslin.

It was that question—or was it a taunt or warning—that had given the metropolis a doomsday complex. It was that awareness of a possible commemorative strike by the .44-caliber killer that prompted the NYPD to mobilize hundreds of uniformed and plain-clothes cops, scores of them as girl-boy decoy teams and dispatched them into the night to seek their elusive prey.

Unmarked cars, trucks, vans, and taxis roamed the streets of the Bronx and Queens with sharp-eyed policemen peering through the windshields into the darkness for a sign of the first outbreak of violence on the street that might have been occasioned by the deadly terrorist.

Policewomen with long brown hair and plainclothes partners sat in cars parked near discotheques and singles bars waiting to lure the man with the fearsome Bulldog to them.

Scores of off-duty policemen volunteered their services and posted themselves at key bridges and highway escape routes to cut off his flight and intercept Son of Sam if he should somehow kill or maim again and elude the many foot and motorized posses prowling the streets for him.

Yet was the killer about to pull off the most daring of stunts—attack on a night when practically all New York knew such extraordinary precautions had been taken by the authorities to capture him? He had only to read the newspapers to know that no sane young woman would go out on a date that night. Let alone cuddle up to her beau in a parked car—on a darkened street.

The killer needed only to have passed by or dropped into a disco or singles bar to see how deserted they were.

Tuning into any radio or TV station could have told him that this was indeed the most dangerous night of all to be out on the street—the most dangerous night especially for Son of Sam, the .44-caliber killer.

He was insane, many experts agreed. But not insane enough to take his chances with that army of trigger-happy lawmen waiting for a confrontation with him.

"Is tomorrow night, July 29, so significant to him that he must go out and walk the night streets and find a victim?" asked Breslin in his column which was headlined, *To the .44-Caliber Killer on His 1st Deathday.* "Or will he sit alone, and look out his attic window and be thrilled by his power, this power that will have him in the newspapers and on television and in the thoughts and conversations of most of the young people in the city?"

If the four stories in the *Daily News* alone weren't enough about the search and preparations to stop the .44-caliber killer if he dared strike on July 29, then certainly Breslin's closing sentence should have kept the killer glued to his "attic window" and shaking in his boots:

"A person who, on any night he goes out, could wind up over the hood of a police car like a deer."

It was a dare the Son of Sam was unwilling to accept. Thus the first anniversary of the death of Donna Lauria and the wounding of Jody Valente passed without a stir from the predator who by now had been truly transformed into a myth.

But for how long would the city be spared from the ravages of this random killer?

One had to wait only a relatively few short hours after the .44-caliber killer's first *Deathday* for the answer...

CHAPTER XIV

BROOKLYN LOVERS: BURNED AND BLINDED

It was on Thursday evening of July 28th in Brooklyn's Sheepshead Bay section. Sixteen-year-old Ricki Moskowitz, who had a remarkable resemblance to Farrah Fawcett-Majors, was having dinner with her sister, Stacy, who was twenty and resembled no one in particular but was a blonde beauty in her own right.

The dinner in Beefsteak Charlie's was a celebration of sorts for Ricki because she'd been invited to audition for TV's Gong Show. Now with desert and coffee finished, Ricki and Stacy paid the check and walked to the entrance.

All at once Ricki's eyes opened wide. She couldn't stop staring at the handsome young man just ahead of them.

She nudged her sister.

"Look, look," she gasped. "He's a living doll ... he looks just like Mark Spitz ..."

With a brashness that she seldom exhibited, Ricki pushed her sister in front of the young stranger so Stacy and he could talk to each other. Ricki herself might have gone for the guy but she knew right away that he was a little too old for her.

Besides, Ricki reasoned, her boyfriend Joe might not like the idea if she did.

Ricki was really thinking of her sister, whom she knew needed an uplifting experience after her bustup with Anthony Robinson who had been engaged to her. This good-looking fellow, she reasoned, might be just the right tonic for Stacy.

As it turned out, Robert Violante was the same age as Stacy—and obviously very much interested in knowing her better. That is, after the formality of introductions.

"How's about the movies Saturday night?" Bob smiled.

"I think I'd like that," Stacy said happily.

She told him where she lived, at 1740 East 5th Street in Brooklyn's Midwood section. He told her that'd be no sweat for him getting there in his father's 1969 Buick Skylark four-door sedan because he lived at 1972 Bay Ridge Parkway, not far at all. Just a mile at most in the western end of Bensonhurst.

They didn't get a chance that night to tell each other much about themselves. But they could do that on their date—and perhaps on other dates, who knew?

But it was a sure thing that Stacy and Bob would like what they heard about each other. Because they were both terrific people.

The brown-eyed, shapely 5-foot-1 inch Stacy was adored by all her many friends. She was a clean cut young woman who disdained bars and took a drink in a discotheque only if she were with a date.

Until seven months ago, she'd been going with Tony Robinson, a six-footer and movie-screen handsome. But then little annoyances and peeves grated on their romance. Stacy called off the engagement.

At home were her father, Jerome, or Jerry as everyone called him, and mother Neysa. They looked after Stacy—and Ricki as much—with warmth, love, affection and attention. A typical Jewish family, they had warmth that was contagious. Not too religious, though. Jerry, the father, who drove a truck for a family ice cream distributing firm, often admitted if he were in temple he wouldn't know what to do. But he believed in God. That was enough for him.

Eight years ago the Moskowitz household was plunged into deepest mourning; a ten-year-old daughter died. She would have been the middle child now had she lived. But time eased the pain of that loss and Neysa and Jerry looked with hope to have Stacy and Ricki grow up, marry nice boys, settle down, and have fine families of their own.

The parents weren't too happy when Stacy interrupted her education by dropping out of Lafayette High School in her junior year. But Stacy had plans. She wanted to work, earn money, and have things. So she attended secretarial school briefly, then took a job as a secretary-receptionist with the Minella Corporation.

Jerry and Neysa weren't disturbed with that. Minella was a family connected shoe business in the Empire State Building. And Stacy loved working there.

"Well," Mrs. Moskowitz said resignedly one day, "maybe Ricki will be the one who goes to college for this family."

Of course it was all too soon to plot Ricki's future. Only eight days ago they had given her a "Sweet Sixteen" party at the house. All the kids were there then.

It had been that way almost all the time at the Moskowitz house; a rallying point for all of Stacy's and Ricki's friends. Anytime they were to go anywhere, the girls and boys gathered on the veranda and plotted their moves.

And the veranda was where Stacy had waited that Saturday evening for Bob Violante to show up and take her on their date. Jerry and Neysa were there too, anxious to meet this handsome young man who was taking their daughter out.

"If he looks like Mark Spitz, as you say," her redhaired, youngish-looking mother nudged Stacy, "then I will let him take me out and you can stay home with your father."

Neysa had yet to meet Bob Violante but that was the sort of reaction he aroused in girls. Invariably the chicks flipped out over the blue-eyed young man's good looks and slender yet rugged physique.

The 6-foot-1 curly-haired, mustached graduate of Brooklyn's New Utrecht High had been looking forward at that plateau of his life for something other than being a clothing salesman at the George Richland Men's Shop on 86th Street and Bay Parkway. He'd been employed there for several months, but Bob never intended that to be his permanent line

181

of work. Actually he wasn't all that sure what he wanted to do in the next job.

However, he was certain of one thing that Saturday night when he said goodnight to his father, Pasquale, known to everyone as Pat, and Mother, Teresa. He was taking Stacy Moskowitz to the Highway Theater to see *New York, New York*, then later, if his date felt up to it, they could drop into Jasmine's, a popular discotheque at 7110 Third Avenue in Brooklyn's Bay Ridge section, which wasn't too far from where Bob worked.

Then who knows what else the rest of the night would hold...?

Shortly before 8 p.m. Robert Violante left his house, got behind the wheel of the car, drove past nearby St. Dominic's Roman Catholic Church, and headed to the tree-lined street where Stacy Moskowitz lived.

He pulled up in front of the house, looked up to the varanda and saw Stacy waving to him. Next to her stood a muscular, powerful-looking man whom Stacy quickly introduced as her father. The woman with the red hair and broad smile was her mother.

"He looks like Mark Spitz, yes," Mrs. Moskowitz said agreeably. "Yes, indeed."

"Have a good time," Jerry Moskowitz called out as Bob escorted Stacy to the car.

They drove to Kings Highway and saw the picture and were let out a few minutes before midnight. Long before in the darkened movie house Stacy had vetoed Bob's suggestion about going to Jasmine's.

They stopped for coffee and a snack instead—and suddenly it was 1:30 a.m.

"Oh," exclaimed Stacy. "I've got to phone my girlfriend Debbie Layne. I'll be right back."

Debra Layne and Stacy Moskowitz were good friends. They hadn't seen each other in some time and only the other day when they met Stacy suggested they doubledate so Debbie could get a look at the handsome Bob Violante. But Debbie's friend wasn't free that night.

However, Debbie and Stacy had agreed, tentatively, to go themselves on an outing to Harriman State Park upstate on Sunday. But only if Stacy confirmed it. That was what the phone call was about.

When Stacy returned, she told Bob everything was arranged. He then paid the check and they went to the car. They drove to the Gravesend Bay waterfront where Bob suggested they could watch the full moon on the water.

He pulled the car into the parking lot of a playground alongside the Shore Parkway at Bay 14th Street. Violante steered his car into a stall alongside an eight-foot-high chain link fence, directly beneath a brilliant sodium-vapor street light.

There were several other cars parked nearby and some of the couples in them took notice of the new arrivals. A playground by day, it served as a popular lover's lane by night.

Bob and Stacy got out of the car and walked hand in hand to a footbridge which crossed over the six-lane roadway, a part of Brooklyn's Belt Parkway, a circumferential artery that courses along the borough's shoreline for some twenty miles.

If the young couple felt any sense of alarm that early Sunday morning about a possible encounter with the dread .44-caliber killer, they certainly weren't showing it then.

Just a few days before, Stacy had bumped into her ex-fiance. They had remained good friends despite their bustup. On that occasion he told her to beware of the .44-caliber killer.

"Don't worry about me," Stacy dismissed Tony Robinson's alert. "He doesn't go after girls with blonde hair."

Perhaps Stacy and Bob didn't believe that the .44-caliber killer could be a menace to them. Not in that far off locale in Brooklyn. They were at least twenty-two miles from the nearest place where Son of Sam had struck.

He had never harmed anyone in Brooklyn, so why start now?

But there was one thing that Stacy and Bob weren't aware of—that the previous Wednesday a man had phoned the Coney Island Precinct and warned:

"This is Son of Sam. I'm going to hit the Coney Island area."

That in essence was the warning which had been phoned to police in Bayside just a few days before Judy Placido and Sam Lupo were shot outside the Elephas Lounge.

Although the greatest concentrations of police on that anniversary weekend were in the Bronx and Queens, the Coney Island area—Bensonhurst and Bath Beach included—also received beefed-up police protection as a result of that phone call.

As a matter of record, a police cruiser had passed the playground area shortly after Stacy Moskowitz and Bob Violante arrived in the parking lot. The patrolmen saw all was quiet and proceeded to other checkpoints.

After crossing the footbridge, Stacy and Bob, still holding hands, walked to the sea wall and glanced out over the water. Glimmering in the bright moonlight were several tankers and freighters at anchor in the bay. From where they stood they could also see the necklace of lights in the distance which illuminated and lent a magical fairyland quality to the towering span of the Verrazzano-Narrows Bridge, the world's longest, which links Brooklyn and Staten Island, the city's fifth borough.

Several minutes later, Stacy and Bob, still holding hands, walked the path back to the footbridge and crossed to the parking lot. Instead of returning to the car immediately, they went to the playground and glided on the swings.

Minutes later, they went back to the car. As they got in, several couples parked nearby spotted a man in his twenties, about 5 feet 8, huskily built, and dressed in blue jeans and gray shirt. He strode from the darkness of the playground, approached the open window on the passenger side of the brown Buick, and pulled a gun.

In the next instant he crouched in the dreaded, now-familiar marksman's pose of the .44-caliber killer, and suddenly there were four successive flashes from the muzzle, followed by the explosive bang, bang, bang, bang.

The man who had fired the gun now, just as quickly as he appeared, turned and walked at a rapid gait along a grassy mall and disappeared into the playground.

Even before the last echo of gunfire had faded a shrill, pleading cry was heard.

"God, I've never done anything. Help me, help me, help me! God, why is this happening? Help me!"

Then followed the incessant sound of the car's horn as Robert Violante, struck by a bullet that entered his temple and exited at the bridge of his nose, collapsed over the steering wheel.

The explosions were heard by Mrs. Dorothy Reback who was up at that hour in her apartment across the way at 1259 Shore Parkway. She went to the window and looked down. She awakened her husband, David, and told him, "Sam did it again!"

Then she dialed the police emergency number 911.

Later she was to give detectives her statement:

"When I looked down the street after the shots, I first saw the tail lights of his (Violante's) car blinking as if he was pushing the brake pedal.

"Then I heard the horn. It was blaring away.

"Then he got out of the car. There was blood all over him. His light blue pants were stained all the way down on one side.

"He leaned against the car for a few seconds. Then he reached out and held himself up against the lamp post. He was yelling, 'Help me, help me!'"

Mrs. Rebeck came downstairs with her husband. Other neighbors who had heard the shots and outcries also responded.

Someone had thought to bring a blanket for the emergency. It was spread on the ground and Violante was made to lie down on it. A towel was rolled up and placed under his head for a pillow.

Someone glanced inside the car, saw Stacy Moskowitz slumped down on the seat but didn't notice any blood on her.

"He's in worse shape than the girl," the witness cried out.

It only seemed that way.

Police Officer Alan Fischer was one of the first patrolmen to arrive. He looked in the car and spoke to Miss Moskowitz. Not yet realizing she'd been shot, Stacy said, "I just got sick in the car..."

But that wasn't the case at all. Stacy had been hit by two bullets. As doctors would soon determine, one bullet grazed her scalp. The other entered the base of her skull, struck a bone, shattered it, and lodged in the cerebellum.

Even as the ambulances arrived to remove the victims to Coney Island Hospital, Stacy Moskowitz was still conscious but rapidly losing awareness. Violante was groggy but still alert.

"I can't see," he cried out. "I can't breathe ...It hurts...My head...My eyes..."

The trip to Coney Island Hospital was so much wasted motion. The facilities were not adequate to handle severe head injuries suffered by Stacy and Bob. The victims were quickly put back into the ambulances and rushed to Kings County Hospital. And there in a scene that had become a monotonously familiar aftermath to the .44-caliber killer's attacks, the victims' families gathered for the first time.

It was 4 a.m. when Jerry Moskowitz burst through the Clarkson Street entrance and hurried toward the emergency room. Flashbulbs exploded and TV camera lights bathed him in a blinding glare. Behind him, struggling to keep up with his hurried pace was Neysa, her hair pulled back, her face ashen, lips trembling. She was leading Ricki, tears running down her cheeks.

"What did they do to my little girl?" Moskowitz cried. He wasn't talking to anyone in particular. "It was a shooting?" he asked. "Who did it...was it that nut?"

Neysa Moskowitz looked around frantically.

"Where is the doctor?" she rasped. "There's got to be a doctor somewhere to tell me what happened to my baby..."

Forty-five minutes passed before the Moskowitzes had any authoritative word about their daughter. It was offered by Dr. S.J. Shahib, who came to America from Pakistan to study medicine and hoped to return there some day to offer his services to his people. Now his job was to inform Stacy's parents as truthfully as he could about her condition.

"She is conscious but we are concerned about the extent of damage to the brain. The wound is critical..."

Five minutes later, a slight, distinguished-looking man walked along the red and black squared tile floor toward the Moskowitzes. As he approached, his step slowed. He seemed to hesitate. A woman was holding dependently on his arm.

Pat Violante and wife Teresa seemed shy to approach the parents of the girl their son had taken on their first date. But then Jerry Moskowitz put out his hand. Suddenly Pat reached out with both hands. The fathers embraced warmly and tears filled their eyes.

"You have such a beautiful boy," Mrs. Moskowitz said to Mrs. Violante. "What beautiful hair and eyes. I was so proud when I saw the both of them leave tonight, a beautiful

189

couple. He looks like Mark Spitz, a real all-American boy..."

Another doctor approached to issue an oral bulletin.

"They are both conscious he said to the parents. They are both reacting with life signs."

The parents sighed with relief. But it was a momentary thing. At 5 a.m. a wheeled stretcher was pushed out of the emergency room bound for the elevator enroute to surgery. A bloodstained sheet covered the form lying limply on the stretcher. He was a young man with a mustache and his head was shaven. Bandages covered his eyes. But Pat Violante recognized his son.

He reached out and touched the hand lying limply on the stretcher.

"Daddy, Daddy, Daddy..." the lips of the patient murmured weakly.

The stretcher disappeared into the elevator. Minutes later a nurse sauntered casually by, a bloodstained brassiere dangling from her hand.

Neysa Moskowitz' face stiffened.

"That's Stacy's bra," she cried. "Look at it. God, no. The blood."

Ricki stiffened her grip on her mother's hand.

"It's not, Mom," Ricki said assuringly. "Stacy's going to be all right."

Pat Violante fought back tears. "I raised my children to be good. They are so good. I've always tried to live the right way. I'm in the auxiliary police. My boy doesn't smoke pot...How can this happen?"

It was Teresa Violante's turn to speak next. It was getting on past 6:30 o'clock. Night had turned into day and still no word from the doctors either about Stacy or Bob.

"It must be bad if they're not telling us anything."

Someone uttered the tired line that no news is good news.

"Remember what the doctor said, they were conscious..."

"No, it's bad, I know..."

Jerry Moskowitz looked at his wife.

"Neysa, I have to call your mother...I have to tell her..."

"Oh, my God...how will you tell her?"

"I'll tell her, please don't worry...I'll be soft..."

Jerry Moskowitz phoned Esther Rome.

"Look...be calm, please...Stacy was in a car accident. She was hurt, but everything is going to be okay..."

Mrs. Rome, who lived a short distance from Kings County Hospital, didn't believe her son-in-law. Her concern about her granddaughter prompted her to speed to the hospital. Her sixth sense drove her there.

"I knew when you called it was that nut," she said after arriving with her husband. "It is no car accident. It is the maniac who is loose who hurt my Stacy..."

It was 7 a.m. now and a hospital supervisor approached the Moskowitzes with a report on

191

their daughter.

"The bullet at the base of the neck is the one we're concerned with. Her skull is fractured."

"Oh, no!" Moskowitz exclaimed. He began to weep. His wife and daughter then started crying fitfully.

The Violantes tried to comfort them.

Minutes later, Dr. Shahib appeared to give a rundown on Bob Violante.

"One eye seems to have collapsed. The other eye is affected but we don't know to what extent..."

Teresa Violante burst into sobs. Her husband embraced her.

She turned herself to the wall and the Moskowitzes moved in. They reached out and all at once the Italian couple were holding hands with the Jewish couple.

Pat Violante was so devastated now that he needed a narcotic to keep him on his feet. An attendant came over and jammed a form in front of the bereaved father to sign so he could be given a sedative. But the attendant wanted to know how much Violante earned per year.

Violante got the narcotic. A while later he seemed to feel a bit better.

Jerry and Neysa Moskowitz had gone home briefly but just before 9 a.m. that Sunday they were back at the hospital.

They were told Stacy went into surgery at 7 a.m. And so had Robert.

Two hours passed. Relatives, friends of both families, and friends of the two young

TWO DONNAS

Donna Laurie was first to die of .44-caliber killer's bullets. Donna DeMasi was lucky to be alive after bullets fractured her collarbone.

I LIVED, I DIED

Carl Denaro survived the killer's attack but he has a plate in his head now. Virginia Voskerichian was coming home from college when she was murdered.

DEATH SPLITS THESE COUPLES

Christine Freund and John Diel (above) planned to marry. She died, he survived. Valentina Suriana and Alexander Esau both were killed.

HAPPY TIMES Blonde Stacy Moskowitz and mother Neysa had no thought of tragedy when this photo was taken

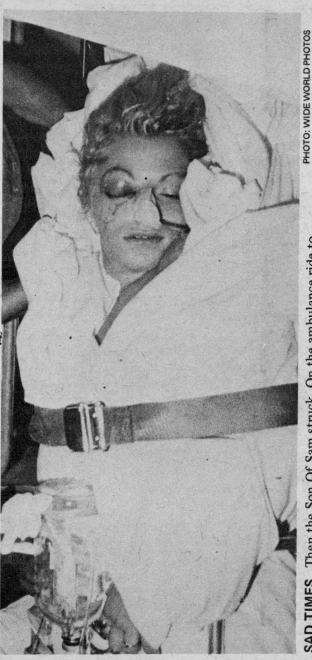

PHOTO: WIDE WORLD PHOTOS

SAD TIMES Then the Son Of Sam struck. On the ambulance ride to the hospital Stacy kept repeating her girlfriend's phone number. Surgery couldn't save her.

DEATH'S AFTERMATH

Robert Violante took Stacy on their first date. He survived but sight's gone. It happened in the car detectives are examining for clues. ____

THE PEOPLE OF THE STATE OF NEW YORK v.

906953 2

LAST NAME   FIRST NAME   INITIAL

STREET ADDRESS

CITY (as shown on license)   STATE   ZIP No.

THE OPERATOR OR REGISTERED OWNER OF VEHICLE IN SHOWN BELOW

| 5 6 1 | X L B | | PASS | 0 4 / 2 7 7 |

FORD   4 DR.

THE PERSON DESCRIBED ABOVE IS CHARGED AS FOLLOWS

7/0   290   BAY 17   K 62

4/3/77   X205   81   B

PROPER   VEHICLE AND   ADMINISTRATIVE   SHER No.
REGULATIONS   TRAFFIC LAW   CODE

FOLLOW INSTRUCTIONS ON REVERSE SIDE

HYDRANT   40

MOTOR VEHICLE TRAFFIC INFRACTION

DESCRIPTION OF TRAFFIC INFRACTION IF NOT SHOWN ABOVE

The person described above is summoned to appear at the
N.Y.S. - DEPARTMENT OF MOTOR VEHICLES
ADMINISTRATIVE ADJUDICATION BUREAU HEARING OFFICE
Located in the County where the summons was issued.
Bronx   Brooklyn   Manhattan
2455 Sedgwick Ave.   350 Livingston St.   50 East 20th St.
Queens   Richmond
1 Lefrak City Plaza   60 Bay Street
(Junction Blvd. & Long Island Expressway)
Daytime hours are Monday through Friday 8:30 A.M. to 4:00 P.M.
Evening hours are Thursday   4:00 P.M. to 7:30 P.M.

DAY OF   19   at

Michael CATANEO   N.Y.P.D.

20   62

TICKET THAT SAVED A CITY

When Police Officer Michael Cataneo wrote out
this summons he had no idea it would help
solve biggest manhunt in NYPD history.

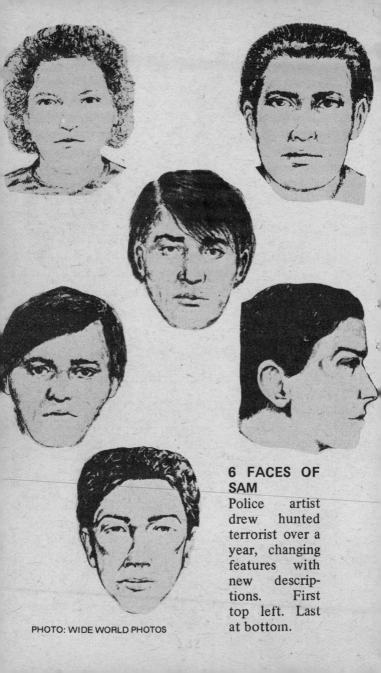

6 FACES OF SAM
Police artist drew hunted terrorist over a year, changing features with new descriptions. First top left. Last at bottom.

PHOTO: WIDE WORLD PHOTOS

THE HUNTED AND THE HUNTER

The search for the .44-caliber killer and his dreaded Bulldog revolver was led by Inspector Timothy J. Dowd.

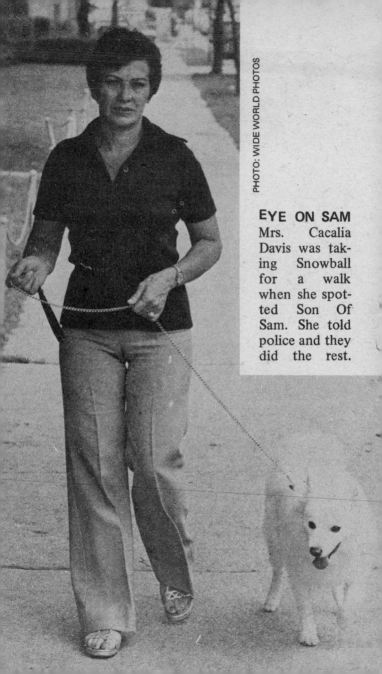

EYE ON SAM

Mrs. Cacalia Davis was taking Snowball for a walk when she spotted Son Of Sam. She told police and they did the rest.

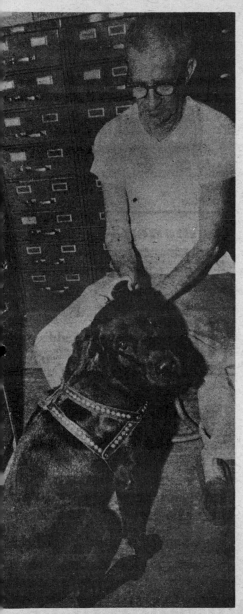

COMMAND TO KILL

Killer said Sam Carr and his Labrador retriever gave him orders to shoot victims.

I want to be free. I will be pretty soon. There is something I must do first. Give me about 58 days for planning.

Iris, do you know what? I'd sure like mankind to be free. Hey love, tell me how to be free, tell me how to find Peace

④

I just might turn out to be one of those unhappy citizens who gave up fighting along time ago, and just fell helplessly into the usual rat-race. Sometimes I feel that the only time peace will come is when I'm dead. But that's not a very much to look forward to.

②

where my weapons were and I told him very politely that I didn't bring them. and I went on to tell him how I felt about carrying and using my weapons. I said, Sir, I politely refuse to carry them because of my moral beliefs and so on.

Well he got kind of pissed off. But, most of all he was surprised. He had no choice except to give me military punishment.

LETTERS FROM A LOVER

While in Army, Iris Gerhardt received many letters from Berkowitz, showing deterioration from drugs.

CAPTURED!

This is the man NYPD seized in Yonkers and booked as Son of Sam, the .44-caliber killer. David Berkowitz was charged with killing six, maiming seven.

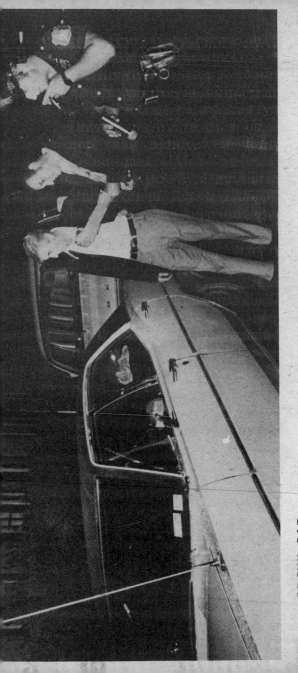

PHOTO: WIDE WORLD PHOTOS

PROWL CAR
Policemen examine Berkowitz's Ford outside his apartment house. It was the car police believe took the .44-killer on his murderous rounds.

THE GUNS OF SAM
Detective Edward Zigo has hands full with .45-caliber submachine gun and long-sought .44-caliber Bulldog which holds Mayor Beam's attention.

PHOTO: WIDE WORLD PHOTOS

POLICE DEPARTMENT

MAID'S NIGHT OUT?

From the time he was a small boy, David Berkowitz was a sloppy housekeeper. His last bedroom shows no effort at improvement.

END OF THE LINE

Detective Zigo leads the prisoner to the last roundup in Brooklyn police station.

victims had streamed into the hospital. Now Stacy's ex-fiance, Tony Robinson, arrived. His chest was heaving with emotion.

"I was once engaged to her...She is a wonderful person, just wonderful. We broke off...but I still love her. That sick sonofabitch who did this, if ever I found him, if ever I got him...he's a gutless coward..."

An attendant came over and handed Pat Violante a bill for the narcotic he was administered.

Steve Dunleavy, a star reporter for the *New York Post* who hails from Australia, the home of his newspaper's publisher Rupert Murdoch tore the bill out of the hospital employe's hand.

"You bloody sonofabitch asshole," Dunleavy screamed, "get your awss off this floor before I throw you into the ether..."

The attendant fled.

It was noon now. Dr. Tarig Siddiqu, a resident in neurosurgery, spoke to reporters.

"In the case of Stacy's injury suffered by her, the statistics, frankly, for survival are not good. The operation has to remove part of the skull casing without damaging the brain. A team of doctors are doing the very best they can."

Jerry Moskowitz later turned to a reporter. "I know...I know...it doesn't look good for her..."

It was early afternoon now, and a priest walked to the Violantes and Moskowitzes, who were seated in the waiting room.

Neysa was the first to speak. "Father, I'm not a Catholic, but will you pray for my daughter? We need all the help we can get."

He comforted Mrs. Moskowitz by assuring her he would pray.

Shortly after 3 p.m. the operation on Robert Violante was over. The doctors sent word that Pat and Teresa could see their son. Pat squeezed Teresa and she smiled wanly.

Then Neysa Moskowitz made a tremendous revelation:

"You know I found out from the police how they knew who Stacy was when they found her on the seat of the car. It so happened that just before the killer hit, she had called her friend Debbie. And then when she was in the ambulance with all those awful things happening to her, she just kept on repeating Debbie's phone number. Then the police called the number and that's how they contacted us. Can you imagine a girl doing that?"

Now shortly after 4 o'clock in the afternoon, Pat and Teresa Violante had seen their son.

"He's alive!" exclaimed Pat Violante after the brief visit to the bedside. "No matter what, he's alive. You have to be thankful for that. He recognized us and talked to us. He said he wanted to go home. He didn't complain. The boy has never had a sick day in his life..."

Violante looked around now.

"Damn!" he exclaimed. "Why isn't Stacy out of the operating room so we can know what's going on...?"

At a few minutes past 4:30 p.m. that Sunday the operation on Stacy was over. The parents were permitted to see her. They were disappointed. Stacy was hooked up to so many machines that her parents weren't certain what was going on.

More than six hours later, they were called back to the hospital. Stacy had already undergone a second operation. The parents, Jerry and Neysea, had no strength left to vent their emotions.

"She's not responding," Jerry Moskowitz cried out after visiting his daughter. "I look at that machine and the lines aren't going up and down."

Neysa wiped her eyes and said, "If she does go, I want her end to have dignity. I don't want her funeral to be a circus. My girl doesn't deserve that."

Stacy Moskowitz survived until 5:22 p.m. Her death followed the last bulletin on her condition which confirmed the hopelessness of keeping the young woman alive.

"We had to take her back to the operating room Sunday night because her pressure was too high," declared Dr. William Shucart, chairman of the Kings County Hospital's Department of Neurosurgery. "The brain fluid which would ordinarily drain off could not escape. That caused pressure to build up and threatened to damage the brain tissue.

"After the second operation, she was returned to intensive care but the brain swelling continued and Miss Moskowitz suffered a series of heart stoppages.

"Medically, we feel helpless. Her brain stem is swollen and there's nothing that can be done to relieve the pressure and pain. She has lost most of her vital functions. Her heart is the only working organ and it had stopped at least six times.

"She has been brought back by the use of electric shocks and drugs.

"The parents have been informed of the situation and they are prepared."

When the end came, Jerry and Neysa Moskowitz were at the hospital. They both broke down and wept, as did Ricki who was at home and heard the news on television.

An hour after Stacy's death, Jerry and Neysa met the press at the hospital. They wanted to express their sentiments—and they spoke from the heart.

Blinking back tears, his voice choked, Moskowitz struggled to read from a prepared statement.

"Although we lost a wonderful daughter, we gained many friends. Everything known to neurosurgeons has been done in an attempt to save her..."

The emotionally swept father then turned to Dr. Shucart who had come to the meeting, too. "I wish to tell everyone who will hear this that Dr. Shucart and all of the staff at this hospital have shown me and my family the greatest consideration I have ever seen."

Neysa Moskowitz, whose composure seemed to hold more stiffly than her husband's, also turned to the physician who had tried his best to save Stacy. "I have never seen such fine professionals as these. There was nothing spared to try and save my daughter."

Then turning away, her thoughts rushed to her daughter.

"She would have been a vegetable if she had lived and she loved life too much for that..."

Now her grief switched suddenly to anger as she spoke about the .44-caliber killer. "An animal like this has to be caught—not to die but to be tortured for the rest of his life. I hope he suffers for the rest of his life. He's not human. I would die right here and now to see this man punished."

A while later a report on Bob Violante's condition was given by the eye specialist who had operated on him, Dr. Jeffrey Freedman. "The left eye suffered damage to the extreme. The bullet entered the left temple and passed through the left eye, shattering it. Only the cornea was left inside the lower lid. The bullet tracked over the nose and exited above the right eyebrow.

"The right eye suffered severe concussion that resulted in a dislocation of the iris, the colored part of the eye. But the full extent of the damage to the right eye cannot be determined yet because the eye is full of blood. We will perform ultrasound tests some days from now to assess whether the retina was damaged."

The question on everyone's lips was answered then by Dr. Freedman. Though the right eye was whole, he said, there was no chance of transplant.

In the minutes after the shooting and for many hours afterward, the police scrambled about frantically in search of the assassin. They threw everyone into the search, roadblocks were set up, cars by the hundreds—especially yellow Volkswagens, since a couple of witnesses thought the assailant fled in one—were stopped and their drivers questioned; every conceivable weapon and tactic at their command was employed.

But Son of Sam, the .44-caliber killer, had eluded the mighty NYPD once more. And with Stacy Moskowitz's death and Bob Violante's blinding, the madman's toll had risen to six killed and seven crippled or scarred. Yet even worse—the police knew nothing more now about the killer than the last time he struck, or the time before, or the time before that....

It was indeed so, as put forth in the big black headline of the *New York Post*:

NO ONE IS SAFE
FROM SON OF SAM

Next day even the usually restrained *Newsday* was swept up by the hysteria:

No Limits Now
To Fear Of Sam

"The illusion of safety is gone," wrote the

Long Island daily's Kenneth Gross. "Now that the killer has struck outside the Bronx-Queens borders, now that it is clear that dark haired women are not the only target, no one feels safe.

"The reaction is no longer isolated. All over the metropolitan area, the fear emerges. Son of Sam has struck a nerve."

Indeed he had struck a nerve. The apprehension spread quickly now into the neighboring suburbs, Nassau County, where Newsday was published, and Westchester County located next to the Bronx.

Police in those counties ordered special briefings for their officers, increased the number of men on patrol, and directed special attention to lovers' lanes where the killer was likely to stalk his victims.

In the city itself, Police Commissioner Codd threw another 120 officers into the hunt for Son of Sam. The number of detectives and other specialists in the search now totalled 300.

Chief of Detectives Keenan went to the Task Force command post in Flushing and reported that police had a much better description of the killer from eyewitnesses at his last foray than any of his others. He said that a police artist would sit down with the persons who saw the gunman and put together a new composite drawing that might more closely resemble the fugitive than the several other sketches being circulated.

The key witness was a young man whom police identified only as Tommy Z. His actual name was withheld in fear that he might become a target of the .44-caliber killer. He was given a 24-hour police guard and moved in protective custody out of his neighborhood.

Tommy Z had been parked with his girlfriend in a car about twenty feet from Bob Violante's car. A movement in his rear view mirror drew Tommy Z's attention—and he watched transfixed at a man approaching the Buick behind.

He could see the two young people in that car but Tommy Z said he was so stupified by the suddenness of what had happened that it didn't occur to him to shout a warning or blow his horn.

As Tommy Z stared in horror, the mysterious figure emerged from the shadows into the light cast by the overhanging light and the full moon. He saw the gray shirt, rolled up sleeves, and the blue jeans. And also the face quite clearly.

"He approached the car slowly," a police spokesman quoted the witness. "He then quickly dropped into a combat-style crouch and fired four bullets through the passenger side..."

He also managed to observe the gunman stand back up, walk away slowly for a few steps, then break into a run and disappear into the shadows.

It was Wednesday after Stacy Moskowitz's

death and the mourners, 275 of them that included parents, relatives, and friends turned out for the final tribute to this beloved girl.

Rain began to fall from the skies which had been leaden all morning as the oak-stained wooden casket was carried from the I.J. Morris Chapel in Flatbush.

The words spoken in his eulogy by Rabbi Solomon Shapiro still echoed: "It is incredible that things like this can happen on the streets of New York. I cannot offer any solace to the family in a tragedy like this."

A police escort then guided the cortege to King Solomon Cemetery in Clifton, New Jersey. Rain continued to fall on the casket which was decorated very simply with a star of David. A grass-colored cloth had been placed now over the coffin as it was carried to the grave.

Neysa Moskowitz reached out and straightened the coverlet on her daughter's casket as Rabbi Shapiro prayed.

"Eternal God Our Creator, we are grateful for the many blessings in the life of Stacy Moskowitz. Bowed by grief in their loss, her family turns to you. Lord of Compassion, reinforce their strength...the Lord giveth, and the Lord taketh away. Blessed be the name of the Lord."

As Stacy was laid to rest beside the grave of her sister Judy Lynn, who had died in 1968 at the age of ten, it was not Rabbi Shapiro's eulogy or his Prayers for the Dead, or

Kaddish, that would echo now.

What was to be of far greater significance was Police Inspector Irving Levitan's declaration while supervising the police detail at Stacy's funeral. "We'll get him. Sooner or later, we're going to get him."

Then the inspector, who is in charge of the Brooklyn South Area where Stacy and her date were shot, looked up at the dark sky and offered a final word.

"It'll probably be some silly traffic violation. They'll bring him in for investigation and it'll turn out to be him..."

CHAPTER XV

THE PARKING TICKET THAT SAVED A CITY

Police Officer William McCormack probably knew the enigmatic Son of Sam, the .44-caliber killer, better than anyone. He had sketched that face a hundred times. Maybe even a thousand. A fifteen-year veteran of the department, McCormack had sat with every surviving victim and every witness and painstakingly developed the information—contour of lips, shape of eyes, style of nose, hairline—that was ultimately incorporated into the various sketches he had drawn.

To be sure, this artist with the NYPD's Identification Section was a dispassionate professional. Emotion or his own personal involvement in the case had no place in his work. And he never allowed such interference to creep in.

The NYPD had issued no fewer than a half dozen of McCormack's finalized sketches over the more than twelve months that the .44-caliber killer had been on the prowl.

Except for just two of those earlier drawings which bore a reasonably strong similarity to each other, all the others varied so drastically that all sorts of speculation were offered to justify the changes.

"He wears a wig," was the most popular theory for the differences in appearance.

But the noses were so different in so many of the sketches. Why? And so were the eyes. The lips, too.

Could there be more than one person? Are there two criminals in a cruel conspiracy to kill and confound the cops? Or more than two—a whole cult of killers, like the Charles Manson devotees? Those were all possibilities that couldn't be discounted. Two or more killers all using the same deadly .44-caliber revolver.

If ever the police—but the public especially—had occasion to wonder about those possibilities it was on August 9th when NYPD artist McCormack's latest sketch of the most wanted man was released.

It had been drawn on the information provided by Tommy Z and others in the parked cars who saw or at least caught a glimpse of the man who shot Stacy Moskowitz and Robert Violante.

When·that sketch hit the street first on the front page of the New York Post that Tuesday, 65,000 Hispanic males and at least 40,000 light-skinned blacks scrambled for cover. They, all of them, looked like the Son of Sam sketch!

You could have seen that face in a thousand different places in the city at any time of day or night. In almost any subway, bus, or wherever.

From a side view not so much, but the full face sketch was definitely a totally different physiognamy than anything anyone had thought the fugitive looked like.

Accompanying explanations were offered by police—that some witnesses, for example, had even been put under hypnosis to make certain they weren't unconsciously suppressing recollections of the killer's appearance. But that didn't reinforce everyone's conviction about the accuracy of the latest version of Son of Sam.

The public was beginning to wonder now more than ever whether anyone knew what the .44-caliber killer really looked like.

But one person who didn't believe she had any doubt at all about what Son of Sam looked like was an Austrian-born woman who lived in a garden apartment on Bay 17th Street— barely a block from the parking lot where Stacy and Bob were shot.

What had given Mrs. Cacalia Davis that gut feeling early Sunday morning was the excitement on the street. She had taken her dog for a walk and everyone was talking about a young couple that had been shot in a parked car by Son of Sam.

That brought memories of an earlier hour that morning rushing back—when she had taken her dog Snowball on another constitutional. It had been very quiet on the street then. It usually was at 2:30 a.m. on Bay 17th Street.

Mrs. Davis had returned home with a friend who'd taken her on a date. He double parked to let Mrs. Davis out because there were no spaces at the curb. As she walked toward her door, she observed a policeman ticketing a car that apparently was parked illegally.

At that hour of the night the most obvious violations a cop can tag a parked car for are being too close to the corner, double parking or blocking a fire hydrant.

Inside her apartment, Mrs. Davis leashed her white spitz and took him out. She walked him and was on the way back to her house when she saw a man walking toward her. She noted that, despite temperatures in the eighties, he was wearing a long-sleeved jacket.

What made her take an even sharper look at the man was the way he was carrying his right arm—very stiffly straight down. And she also detected an object gripped in his hand and hidden partly up his sleeve.

As he neared her, Mrs. Davis became apprehensive. He was a stranger and his gait disturbed her. He had catlike movements.

Mrs. Davis hesitated going to her door. She wanted that weird character to disappear first so he wouldn't see where she lived. In a few seconds it was over. He gave her a sharp look and glanced down at her dog as he went by. Mrs. Davis turned around and saw him walk into a courtyard. He was soon out of sight.

Later that Sunday, in mid-morning, Mrs. Davis went out with Snowball again. The first couple she bumped into asked if she had heard about the shooting.

"Oh, so that was what the noise last night was," Mrs. Davis said.

Before she'd fallen asleep, Mrs. Davis heard

a loud noise that she thought might be a car backfiring. Then she heard a horn blaring incessantly. That made her suspect a car burglar alarm had been triggered. When sirens sounded still later, she assumed the police had responded to a car burglary.

When the couple told her the shooting was the work of Son of Sam, the .44-caliber killer, Mrs. Davis blurted that she had seen him earlier that morning. But the couple simply laughed—and that was the last time she spoke about the stranger that day.

But by the next day, Monday, Mrs. Davis was seized with terror. After reading the newspapers and hearing accounts of the crime on radio and TV, the horrifying thought occurred to her that the .44-caliber killer might come stalking after her because she had seen him.

That night, she went to see her friend Tina and her husband Steve and told them. Steve asked why Mrs. Davis hadn't gone to the police. She replied that it was for the same reason that she came to them—fear.

But the couple assured Mrs. Davis the police would never reveal her identity. The next morning, Tina phoned the 10th Homicide Zone at the Coney Island Precinct. Detective Joseph Strano took the call. The tall, wavy-haired, soft-spoken policeman listened to Tina and his pulse quickened.

"Give me your address and I'll be right over," he said urgently.

The thirty-five-year-old detective, on the

force fifteen of those years, informed his boss, Detective Sergeant James Shea, what he was doing then drove his Rambler to Bay 17th.

Tina and Steve introduced themselves, then Mrs. Davis. But it wasn't as easy as Strano had thought to get the information he came for. Mrs. Davis was still terrified. Would she at least look at the sketches Strano had brought with him?

"I saw them in the newspapers," Mrs. Davis said in her Austrian accent. "They are not much like him. The man I saw is different."

Could he bring a police artist to the house, the detective wanted to know? With Mrs. Davis' vivid recollection of his face, a more accurate sketch might be drawn.

No! No! No!

Strano became a psychologist now. He appealed to Mrs. Davis' reason. He tried to stir her emotions. Her sense of civic duty—where was it? Why in the first place did she phone the police if she didn't intend to go through with her identification of the man who was killing and maiming all those young people?

"I didn't phone, Tina did."

"But you consented to the call."

And so it went, back and forth for something like five hours. Then...

"All right. I'll see the artist."

Officer Bill McCormack came over from Manhattan with his sketch pad and drawing pencils. He listened to Mrs. Davis and he drew lines. Gradually they shaped a face. He showed it to Mrs. Davis.

"He looks Puerto Rican," she told McCormack. "The man I saw wasn't Puerto Rican-looking."

McCormack went into another sketch, then another, finally still another—until the witness agreed that the last version was the closest thing to the man she saw.

Strano thanked Mrs. Davis profusely for her assistance and went back to the police station.

"How's it look?" Sergeant Shea looked up at Strano.

"I think there just may be something there," the detective said. "But when it comes to the sketch bit, I don't know. All it'll be is another sketch."

"Then what makes you think there's something there, Joe?" Shea demanded.

"I got a hunch on something, that's why I'm up like I am. Let me check with the uniformed guys...."

Strano remembered what Mrs. Davis had said about a cop writing out a traffic ticket at 2:30 a.m.

Strano and two other detectives assigned by Shea to help went through all the traffic tickets that cops in Coney Island gave out that early Sunday morning. It wasn't such a monumental task to find the tickets issued in that area of Bensonhurst because, after all, after 2:30 a.m. no cop in the entire NYPD had time to write out a traffic summons. Not when the shooting of Stacy Moskowitz and Robert Violante commanded such extreme priority to find the .44-caliber killer.

The search quickly yielded three traffic tickets issued in the area surrounding the crime scene. Within minutes the identities of the three errant motorists were in police hands from the Motor Vehicle Bureau. Two of the motorists turned out to be respectable citizens from the neighborhood. They better have been because they were both in their sixties.

But the third—well, now that was worth a check.

"Mmmmm," mused Shea when Strano put the summons numbered 906953 2 on the sergeant's desk.

"I wonder what good citizen David R. Berkowitz of Yonkers was doing in our neck of the woods at oh-two-hundred hours?" Shea asked.

"You got every right to ask that, Jim," Strano smiled.

"Then I'll tell you what you do, babe," Strano rasped. "You get on the horn to Yonkers and see if they got a line on this bird. But, hey, don't give them anything."

"Are they working up in Yonkers or are they still out with picket signs?" Strano asked snidely. Yonkers cops had been pulling work action in recent times over cutbacks in the force and other grievances.

"Why don't you make a free call and find out," Shea said more snidely.

Fifteen minutes later, Strano returned to Shea. The grin on Strano's face was ear to ear.

"Let me feel your pulse," Shea said.

"Oh, man, what's a third-grade detective like me doing with such a big one?" Strano said.

"Because God looks after those of us who aren't capable enough to work for the Task Force," Shea shot back. "Now tell me what you got...."

"I'm about to be a great big hero, Jim. Because our David Berkowitz is right out of the loony bin. Yonkers tells me he's got no record—but what a career he's made out of busting balls."

"Stop breaking mine, Joe, and tell me what he's done," Shea interrupted.

"He writes crazy letters, he threatens people, sends postcards, everything anonymous. He's the local cuckoo."

"Hey," Shea almost jumped out of his chair, "this sounds real good. How about going up there with Zigo and Longo and see what you come up with?"

"You mean you don't want the experts in Flushing to have this?" Strano smiled.

"Oh, they're so busy chasing all those good leads, I think maybe we should help them out," Shea smiled. The tone was very, very sarcastic.

Before leaving for Yonkers, Strano, along with Detectives Edward Zigo and John Longo went to speak with Police Officer Michael Cataneo who wrote the ticket for the four-door white Ford sedan with the license 561-XLB for blocking a hydrant in front of 290 Bay 17th

Street—the very block where Mrs. Davis said she spotted the man she believed might be Son of Sam!

They wanted to know if Cataneo, or his partner, Officer Jeffrey Logan, had seen any suspicious character around at that hour. Of course the detectives didn't expect them to say they had, for if they indeed had seen such a person they would have stopped and questioned him, then reported it to the squad.

"I didn't see anybody on the street except one car that stopped near us on 17th and let a woman out," Cataneo explained. "Then right after I wrote the ticket and went back on patrol, we got the call on the shooting..."

Cataneo drove his police cruiser as escort for the ambulance which took Stacy to the hospital and Logan rode inside the ambulance with her.

Anything else?" Cataneo asked.

"Yeah," Strano said quietly, "go light a candle for a very nice lady on Bay 17th."

"Who's that?" Cataneo asked puzzled.

"I'll let you know, I'll let you be the first to know, Mike," Strano said. "You're going to be a big man before this is over. In fact, I feel it's bigger than all of us put together..."

"Say hello to Pete Intervallo and Tom Chamberlain," said Mike Nobotny, the supervising sergeant, introducing the Yonkers cops to the three detectives who had travelled by car just a kilometer or so further than that 26-mile subway ride from Coney Island to Van

228

Cortlandt Park in the Bronx.

Intervallo and Chamberlain closeted themselves with Strano, Zigo, and Longo. The Yonkers detectives ran down everything they had on David Berkowitz—the letters he was suspected of having written to Sam Carr, the shooting of his dog, the crazy condolence card sent to Jack Cassara in New Rochelle, the suspicion that Berkowitz sent the hard-of-hearing lady a note and the killing of the superintendent's children's dog on Buhre Avenue in the Bronx...

"This guy is out of it," Longo said. "Have you questioned him at all?"

"He's too smooth," Chamberlain explained. "Nobody knows for sure it's him."

"How about the letters," Zigo said. "Check on the writing?"

"We're trying to get some samples of his penmanship," Intervallo put in. "Then we can compare. We were expecting to pick up something this afternoon."

"How come you guys didn't give this to the NYPD?" Strano asked with a smile. "Wanna catch Son of Sam all by yourselves?"

Intervallo and Chamberlain looked at each other. They broke into uproarious laughter.

"Shall I tell 'em?" Intervallo said finally.

"Be my guest," Chamberlain winked. "But break it easy, Pete. You shouldn't shock our visitors..."

Intervallo proceeded to tell the detectives from Coney Island about their encounter with the man from the NYPD's Intelligence Division, Richard Salverson.

"We gave him everything we had," Intervallo said. "As a matter of fact the only thing he didn't get was that Berkowitz apparently has a hard-on for another tenant in the building—a deputy sheriff from Westchester. Not only is he sending notes but we think he set a little fire outside that poor hump's door last Saturday…"

"Yeah, and with .22s thrown in for good measure," Chamberlain interrupted.

"You guys got any ideas what the man from I.D. did with the poop you gave him?" asked Longo.

"I'm really dumb when it comes to that," Intervallo said. "For all I know he could have been giving us a hand job when he said he was going to pass it on to Dowd's guys."

"Oh, hold on," Chamberlain broke in. "The best is yet to come. Last week, just after the girl and fellow were shot, Sam Carr took a drive out to Flushing and visited the Task Force."

"What for?" Strano asked, puzzled.

"To tell them about Berkowitz…to ask them when the hell they were going to move on him," Intervallo said.

"What was he told?" Strano asked.

"That they were going to look into it," Intervallo answered. "In fact that's what we thought when you fellows dropped in—that you were from the Task Force."

"Oh, we don't rate that high," said Strano. "But thanks just the same for thinking of us
230

with such reverence..."

It was now 4:30 p.m. of Wednesday, August 10th.

Task Force had been informed about the swift series of developments that had apparently brought the thirteen-month pursuit of the .44-caliber killer to a seeming climax.

Of course, Commissioner Codd and Chief of Detectives Keenan—even Mayor Beame—were notified about the impending break. They were informed downtown—by sources unknown—just so the bigshots would know who should get the credit for the collar when it happened.

Detectives Strano, Zigo, and Longo were not to be denied. They were assigned with a team of fifteen detectives that also included Edward Blasie and Ed O'Sullivan from Coney Island, to go to Yonkers and bring in Berkowitz.

After search warrants for the suspect's car and apartment were obtained, the cops moved in. Chief Keenan, Inspector Dowd, and Captain Borrelli headed the NYPD contingent. In Yonkers they were augmented by a dozen men from that city's police force.

They posted themselves as inconspicuously as they could in every strategic location on Pine Street and all cross streets in the neighborhood to seal off all possible routes if the suspect tried to flee.

The stakeout was not many minutes old when detectives spotted a white four-door

Ford sedan, a Galaxie, with the license 561-XLB. The car was parked almost in front of 35 Pine Street where Berkowitz lived.

The car was locked but through the window the detectives saw the stock of a rifle sticking out of a duffle bag on the back seat. They saw other things. On the front seat were maps, an automobile distributor cap and the parking ticket Officer Cataneo had slapped on the windshield.

It was deemed too risky to knock on Berkowitz's 7-E apartment door. No telling whether he'd chance a shootout with the cops. The decision was made to wait. And wait is what the police did.

Just before 10 p.m., Berkowitz walked out of the apartment. It was dark but almost every sleuth on the stakeout recognized the man they had been waiting for. A description had been provided by Officers Intervallo and Chamberlain, under whose surveillance the suspect had been all those many months.

He walked to his car. As he unlocked the door and begun to squeeze in behind the wheel, three detectives who'd been sitting in a parked car, leaped out and pounced on him. One put a gun to his head.

"Freeze!" he shouted.

He ordered Berkowitz to get out and spread himself against the car. As he got out, the suspect curled his lips into a sickly smile.

"Well, you got me..." he murmured.

Then with inordinate speed he was frisked, his hands were handcuffed behind his back, and he was led to a police cruiser. Then he was driven to police headquarters in Manhattan where he was ushered through several score reporters and photographers in a brilliant bath of flashing and constantly burning lights.

After walking the gauntlet of clicking shutters and whirring cameras with seeming ease, he was escorted into an elevator which whisked him up to Keenan's office. Meanwhile, other detectives carried the paraphernalia they found in his car, as well as apartment.

There were many items that would need recording on the evidence sheet—a submachine gun, rifle, many boxes of all caliber ammunition, and a manila envelope with familiar hand-lettering with the serifs slanted at 45-degree angles. Inside was a message that had been sent to the deputy sheriff in Berkowitz's building, starting, "Because Craig is Craig so must the streets be filled with Craig (death)..."

But the most telling evidence, found under the front seat of the car, was a weapon with a high luster police blue finish, an American walnut hand-checkered Bulldog grip, a partridge type 9/64-inch front and square notched rear sight, and a wide trigger and hammer, chrome-moly steel frame, an unbreakable firing pin, and transfer bar ignition.

The weapon was 7½ inches in overall length, 4½ inches high, its barrel 3 inches in length, and it was a 5-shot, double action revolver. Fully loaded, too!

It was a .44-caliber Charter Arms Bulldog revolver—and when it was tested later by ballistics it was the very gun that killed six, maimed or scarred seven, and terrified millions in the dread reign of the Son of Sam, the .44-caliber killer....

THE ACCUSED: SON OF SAM'S OWN STORY

BOOK TWO

CHAPTER XVI

BORN TO BE GIVEN AWAY

He was born in Brooklyn on June 1st, 1953 and named David Richard Falco. But his parents, Tony and Betty Falco, never changed his diaper or even warmed a single nursing bottle for him. David Richard was taken from the hospital by Nathan and Pearl Berkowitz to their small apartment at 1105 Stratford Avenue in the Bronx. They were the ones who gave the infant all the loving care, treatment and affection a newborn baby must have.

Eighteen months later, on November 30, 1954, in the courtroom of Bronx Surrogate Christopher C. McGrath, Betty Falco signed away all rights as a parent of little David Richard. An agreement was drawn up making Nathan and Pearl Berkowitz his adoptive parents.

David's early growing-up years were marked by pampering that was to the extreme. That was understandable since Nathan, who made a comfortable living as a hardware store owner, and his wife, Pearl, had been childless for the many years of their marriage. Nathan was forty-three years old then, Pearl a buoyant thirty-eight but unable to conceive.

The six-story red brick apartment house where David Richard was brought and where his parents had lived since 1947 was inhabited almost entirely by Jewish families. The neighborhood and for miles around still had the ethnic mixes of Italians, Irish, Poles, Germans, Greeks and other nationalities which seemed to complement each other—until the Hispanics cascaded into the Bronx and triggered the mass exodus of the others. But in 1953, in that particular area—Stratford Avenue—the Jewish residents were the predominant ethnic and religious group.

In his early years, young David Richard Berkowitz always accompanied his mother and father to synagogue on the High Holy Days. On Yom Kippur, the Day of Atonement and most sacred of holy days for Jews, his parents would take young David between them, each holding a hand, and walk the six short blocks on Westchester Avenue, under the IRT local's Pelham Bay line elevated structure, to the Bronx River.

They would stand on the bridge where Whitlock Avenue and Freeman Street and West Farms Road almost met, long before the neighborhood was ripped up to build the Sheridan Expressway. And from the bridge railing the Berkowitzes would cast their sins into the water.

Eating out was the most enjoyable pastime that Nathan and Pearl Berkowitz knew of. And of course their young son thrilled to the prospect of dining out with his mommy and daddy.

The most frequent excursions were to the Crown Restaurant, on Westchester Avenue just two stores down from the corner of Elder

Avenue. Now and then they dared to eat in a non-kosher eating place called Jack's Open Kitchen, across from the Crown.

When the mood moved Nat and Pearl, they'd hop aboard the Westchester Avenue bus which had started to run not too long ago, after the trolleys had been retired. They'd ride for five minutes to Southern Boulevard, then get off and walk to the Hunt Points Dairy, just opposite the Loew's Spooner Theater.

And there they'd feast on a meatless nine-course meal that cost $1.80 apiece. With the generous 75-cent tip that Nathan, the father, always left at the table for the tuxedo-ed waiter, the tab seldom exceeded seven dollars, tax included.

What a treat it was for David after the meal at the Hunts Point Dairy when his father had already suggested at the table during the middle of the meal, "How about the movies after dinner...?"

"Daddy...daddy...yes, yes," young David would squeal delightedly.

Then there'd be a choice. It could be the Spooner across the street, or even the Star almost next door to the restaurant which always showed not two but three features. Or they could really live it up by going to the Loew's Boulevard down the street a bit, a short distance past all the big shops on the busy boulevard. That was where the big movies from Metro Goldwyn Mayer and Paramount and Warner Brothers always played a week before they hit the Spooner.

For variety sometimes the Berkowitzes went to the Leff's Freeman, which wasn't close to home and which didn't screen first-run films—but it played pictures sometimes that Nat and Pearl Berkowitz had missed and wanted to see.

Closer to home, they also had the Ward Theater, on Westchester Avenue. In fact, the Ward was the theater where David Richard Berkowitz went on Saturday afternoons with his twenty cents, after he was old enough to go to the movies by himself.

David Richard seemed to be a normal boy during those years. Of course there were times when he was rambunctious, when he brawled with kids on the street, when parents complained to Pearl that her son was a "no-goodnick" or a "rotten child" or whatever other aspersions were cast. But in the main, David Richard was a kid who seemed to fit into the society where he was growing up.

His early schooling started with kindergarten at Public School 77, at Ward Avenue and 172nd Street, just opposite James Monroe High School which a short decade before had been known as the world's most populous high school. It had 12,000 students—although lower classes were spread out on the top floors of a half-dozen elementary schools in the East Bronx that served as annexes.

That was how it all began for David Richard Berkowitz. But his school life and his life at home were fated to take different courses...

CHAPTER XVII

A SHY, INTROVERTED
SCHOOLBOY

There'd been considerable confusion and dissension about the motivations and direction of young David Richard Berkowitz as he grew into a young schoolboy.

As Mrs. Lillian Goldstein, a Stratford Avenue neighbor whose two sons played with David, put it:

"He was a hyperactive child and his parents had a difficult time with him. Kids would complain that he hit them without reason. His parents were nice and they gave him the kinds of toys any child would cherish. More for sure than any kid in the neighborhood."

One story that went the rounds after David Berkowitz was arrested as the .44-caliber killer was that he had a yellow auto dashboard toy as a child of five or six, that it was on a kitchen table, and while he was driving behind the steering wheel David had turned to the kid with him and said, "Do you want to join my girl-hating club?"

"He was a handful," Mrs. Goldstein observed. "His mother was taking him to psychiatrists. He did a lot of very strange things. He would push people. He always had a vivid imagination, but what he would say was a little beyond what the average child would say. His mother would laugh and smile."

When he was four-and-a-half someone, nobody knows who, hurled a rock from what was probably the roof of an apartment house on Stratford Avenue. The rock caught David Richard on the head. His foster mother took him to Westchester Square Hospital where David was patched with five stitches.

David was five years old now and the Goldsteins decided to avail themselves of a new phenomenon in urban residential living—low-cost city housing. But they were thwarted from taking their little pup, Lucky, a mutt they had picked up in a snowbound vacant lot six months earlier. The covenants of the project prohibited pets. So the Goldsteins left the dog with the Berkowitzes in hopes that a deep-rooted love between dog and boy might be born.

But that relationship between Lucky and David Richard never developed. And ultimately the dog was disposed of to the ASPCA. David Berkowitz didn't like dogs.

Nobody knows that better now than Sam Carr does.

"Some people remember David as a superb baseball player and power hitter, given to passions to which he would devote incredible energy..."

That was the way another neighbor remembered David. But if the boy had ever hoped to follow in the footsteps of the Detroit Tigers' great Hank Greenberg or the Mets' mighty Ed Kranepool, Berkowitz did not attend his neighborhood's James Monroe High School which was that slugging duo's alma mater.

By the time he was ready for high school, David was living in another neighborhood and was required to attend Christopher Columbus.

Besides P.S. 57, David also went to Junior High School 123 at 1025 Morrison Avenue before he was ready for Columbus.

One of his classmates in elementary school, Gwendolyn Bellamy, recalled what David was like.

"He was a strange kid," Miss Bellamy remembered. "I met him the first time in third grade. He was pretty nice but if he did anything wrong in class he'd stand very quiet, head bowed while the teacher bawled him out.

"One time Miss Drucker pulled his ear and he still didn't say a word. He only cried."

Gwen and David were in different 4th and 5th grades but met again in a special sixth-grade class for music-oriented pupils.

"When I saw him in the class," Miss Bellamy chuckled, "I said, 'David, what are you doing in here? You don't have an ear for music!'"

The shy, introverted boy just shrugged. And that year of 1965, David Berkowitz was the bane of Miss Auerbach's existence.

"He really raised hell," Miss Bellamy recalled. "He was constantly coming to class late. Sometimes he'd say, 'I was at the candy store, that's why I'm late.'"

When Miss Auerbach called for his homework, more often than not David didn't have it.

"There was never a reply from David," Miss Bellamy said. "He'd merely tap his hand on the desk, run his other hand through his hair and hem and haw."

Once Miss Bellamy remembered that David blew his cool at the teacher who was scolding him.

"Why don't you stop picking on me ... I'm sick and tired, stop it!" he shouted.

After graduation, Gwen went to different junior and senior high schools. Then, in 1975 when she was attending Bronx Community College whom did she bump into on campus?

"David Berkowitz," she said she shouted to the young man in the green Army jacket. "P.S. 77!"

"Gwendolyn Bellamy, P.S. 77!" he smiled back.

Seeing Miss Bellamy then may have brought memories of his early childhood years soaring back. Memories in the beginning of an all-Jewish neighborhood where he was like everyone else as far as religion and mores were concerned.

He may also have remembered how the neighborhood started to change, and finally became so totally different that it made flight to new surroundings imperative. In this altering environment David was being teased. The newcomers were calling him "fat

Jew-boy" and other such derogations.

Joe "Ice" Phillip who knew David from as far back when Gwendolyn Bellamy knew him, in the third grade, remembers that when the new kids got on David's back, he went into a shell.

"He kept it inside, but I could tell the name-calling got to him..."

Joe and David got along because, as Phillip explained it, "I was small and skinny and the other kids teased me, too."

As he retreated from reality, David Richard also abided by a strange inner calling. At times, for no reason at all, he'd bust out in uncontrollable laughter. Then at other times he'd rant and rave, again for no special reason.

His belligerence and rebelliousness against authority was roaring up toward the much higher peak to be reached after those early years on Stratford Avenue.

David Margolies, now a stockbroker but then a music teacher, made the journey to the sixth floor of 1105 Stratford Avenue every week for a year. His job was teaching the tall, handsome, wavy-haired youngster the saxophone.

"He had no talent for it," Margolies said. "I told his mother so many times, 'Pearl, he will never learn. He doesn't have an ear for it. Give it up. You are wasting your money...'

"Yes, he was terrible. But the music was the least of it.

"One time I went into the house and he was

throwing a tantrum. Tearing curtains off the wall, throwing pictures, screaming, and kicking. I said I'd come back later.

"He used to make his mother cry terribly. The tantrums, his arrogance was something else. He was the most erratic kid I've ever known."

The adoption papers formalized by Justice McGrath had declared in the court's stilted legalistic language that "the minor, Richard David Falco shall be henceforth regarded and treated in all respects as the child of said Nathan Berkowitz and Pearl Berkowitz, his wife, and be known and called by the name of David Richard Berkowitz."

But the kids in the neighborhood, clinging to the worst cruelty, wouldn't let young David Richard Berkowitz be who he was. They taunted him about his adoption.

Once when he was about eleven, even a grown woman descended to the gutter as she scolded the boy:

"You're a fresh kid. I know why, too. That's not your real mother and father. You're adopted..."

There were times, according to Margolies, when David himself took umbrage at his mother for no particular reason and threw his heritage up at her.

"He'd curse her because he knew he was adopted," said Margolies.

David's stepfather, according to Margolies and many others, was a gentle, kindly man. But Nathan Berkowitz also knew how David behaved toward his stepmother when the father was away. Yet he did little to straighten out the boy.

"Nat pampered the kid too much, just like the mother," one former neighbor remembered.

Yet from what could be recalled collectively about the Berkowitz household and family life, Pearl Berkowitz was considered more the disciplinarian than Nat, however little her clout apparently was.

But by now—in the mid-1960s—Pearl was no longer strong and vigorous as she once had been. A lump had been detected in her breast. A radical mastectomy was performed. A couple of years later, another cancerous growth was discovered in her other breast. Again she went under the knife. Pearl Berkowitz had little time left now.

The neighborhood was changing much faster now and it was too many flights for his wife to climb to the sixth floor. Nat wanted to make his wife's last months as easy as he could.

They had been building Co-op City at the time and he had asked Pearl if she would like to move there. She agreed and volunteered to fill out the application. In it she wrote:

"We are most anxious to move into Co-op City."

She stated her husband's income was "under $16,000."

By then Nat Berkowitz's fortunes were on the decline. His hardware store in the once-thriving business section of Gun Hill Road, between Jerome and Webster Avenue, fell off precipitately as the neighborhood changed.

A friend, Nathan Vogel, who also had a hardware store on White Plains Road, between 213th and 214th Street, also felt the pinch of changing neighborhoods. He suggested to Berkowitz that they open a store together in the busy South Bronx, at Melrose Avenue and 158th Street. It was a prosperous neighborhood, with Italian, Jewish, and German families comprising the core of the ethnic mix there.

This was still a time before Pearl's illness. A time of joy and happiness—a time for David Richard's assent to manhood. His Bar Mitzvah.

The ceremony was held on Saturday morning, June 4th, in Adah Israel Temple at 2075 Grand Concourse. Nowadays the worshipers who enter that building's doors are Seventh Day Adventists.

As he grew older, David's deportment remained a problem. Just six months before he had become a man in the Jewish tradition, David Richard celebrated New Year's Eve at the Stratford Avenue apartment with a party. Friends dropped over and the noise was something fierce. A woman downstairs rapped on the door and asked for quiet. There was no response from inside, only muffled giggles.

By the time she returned to her apartment, David gave her a reply. As a child, David had developed a fetish about his physique. He wanted muscles. And he wanted his mucles to have muscles. So he got a set of barbells. And that was how he answered the downstairs woman's plea for quiet. He dropped the barbells on the floor. Then he and his friends exited through the bedroom window to the fire escape and raced downstairs screaming away in triumph.

Fifteen months after his Bar Mitzvah, David Berkowitz lost the one person he truly loved but whose life all too frequently he had made miserable. Pearl Berkowitz had lost her battle to cancer on October 5, 1967.

At the funeral the next day, David did something no one had seen him do. No one thought him capable of it. He cried.

Nineteen months later, the apartment in Co-op City that Pearl had applied for was ready for occupancy. A still-saddened Nathan Berkowitz and his sixteen-year-old son bade farewell to their old neighborhood, completely deteriorated, decaying, and filth-ridden. They moved into a sparkling new two-bedroom apartment—No. 17-B, at 170 Dreiser Loop. Berkowitz had paid $2,025 down for the ownership he shared with the many other thousands of tenant-investors moving into the Bronx's new residential paradise.

David had finished the 9th grade at J.H.S. 123 the previous June and that September had begun the 10th grade at Christopher Columbus High.

David Ratner was one of the young men

who could still see David in secondary school:

"I remember him in a few of my classes. I think in two gym classes, and I'm almost positive in a hygiene class.

"He was like a child. He wasn't retarded, just very immature, the kind of guy who would sneak into a locker room or steal a ball from you and dribble.

"You'd have to ask him to get it back. He was the kind of guy who would push you when you were jumping to shoot.

"He was very physically strong. He would constantly, with two or three other guys, be lifting weights. But he was about 5 feet 8 or 5 feet 9 then. He had stopped growing."

As Ratner recalled, David also picked friends who were younger and smaller than he.

In his middle teens David's personality became stranger, his behavior even more erratic. He would go off by himself, disappear for days at a time. When he'd return, he'd offer no explanation of where he had gone. At most he'd only say, "I just took a walk..."

In retrospect, that disappearing act was, much of it, attributable to certain disturbing developments at home. Disturbing to David, that is.

In his loneliness, Nathan Berkowitz had joined a singles club in Co-op City. The members were mostly middle-aged parents without partners. During his socializing there he met Julia, who was about five years younger than Pearl would have been then.

The possibility of marrying Julia coursed through Nat's mind. But he wanted advice. He went to his partner and friend, Nat Vogel, who said:

"I told him, 'Listen, when Pearl was alive, you did everything you could to help her. She's dead now. It wasn't like you had another woman on the side. You shouldn't feel guilty. Marry Julia!'"

And so in 1971 Nat and Julia were married—much to David Richard Berkowitz's displeasure. He felt Julia was intruding on his life but especially she was stomping on the fond memories he held for his dead mother, Pearl.

David also felt Julia married his father for his money—because his new stepmother bought all new furniture for the apartment. His new stepmother also brought a teenaged daughter to live in the house and that displeased David to no end.

One of the first things Julia's daughter did was hang a large impressionistic painting she had executed on the living room wall.

"The mother was always showing it off," a friend of David's said. "She was always bragging how wonderful her daughter was as a painter. One day Dave turned it upside down and she never even noticed the difference. It stayed that way. He used to get a big kick out of that."

That happened after the stepsister had gone off to California for some commune experiences. Before she left David's experiences

251

with his stepsister were constant nightmares.

"Her mother was always comparing the stepsister to David. She was always going on about how her daughter was so great, how she was a tremendous painter, and how Dave wasn't even going to college.

"He didn't like the girl no how. In fact he disliked her a whole lot and hated her friends. Whenever they came over he'd leave the house and complain to his friends that they were a 'bunch of yentas.'"

If having his son's animosity to contend with in the house wasn't enough for Nathan Berkowitz now, other problems were rearing up with sudden swiftness.

Business at the hardware store had gone into a tailspin. By 1972 the fires that were beginning to burn stores and tenements in the South Bronx started to encroach on Melrose Avenue. The arsonists were getting too close for Nat Berkowitz's comfort.

He had already had one scare that took years off his life. A holdup in the store at gunpoint. Never had that happened to him before. Never again would it happen. Nat Berkowitz vowed that day. He retired from the business.

The robbery and the changing neighborhood weren't the only reasons he had decided to take up a life of ease under the Florida palms. Even the unpleasantness of a grumpy son at home wasn't the reason Nat Berkowitz decided to move with Julia to Boynton Beach. He also found he had diabetes.

By 1975 Nathan Berkowitz was sixty-five years old. How many more years was he going to live? So, everything combined to make Nat Berkowitz and Julia Berkowitz former Co-op City dwellers.

Their leaving didn't wipe the doorbells clean of Berkowitzes in the project. For, on one of the floors below 17-B lived Nat Berkowitz's mother, David's grandmother, Mrs. Rose Berkowitz. She was eighty-four, yet except for some deafness she was still vigorous and strong. In another apartment in the same building lived a sister of Mrs. Berkowitz, David's grand aunt.

But it wasn't Nat or Julia or the grandmother or the aunt whom the neighbors remembered most vividly. It was David Richard. Especially was he remembered by Mrs. Shirley Schilkraut, who back in 1970—a short time after David Richard and his father moved into 170 Dreiser Loop—had some smoke coming out of her kitchen.

David Berkowitz, who had had a desire to be a fireman throughout his childhood, responded to Mrs. Schilkraut's problem as though it were a five-alarmer.

"I had left a pot cooking and went across the street to my sister's house," recalled Mrs. Schilkraut, a chill still running through her as the memory surges back. "It was Heinz baked beans and I guess David must have smelled them burning."

"When I came back I found the wall already broken. He did it with a hammer and stuff so he could put his fist through to open the knob.

"I said, 'You should have called the fire department. You didn't have a right to break my wall.'

"All he said was he was sorry."

Mrs. Schilkraut could also remember that David was "different" in many other ways.

"He never looked you straight in the face, he always kept his head down. He was quiet and he kept to himself. His room was sloppy, like a boy keeps his room, but Julia kept the rest of the apartment immaculate.

"But I always had that feeling about him ... I didn't want to be alone with him ..."

Neighbors who rode in the elevators with David remembered that he seldom acknowledged their presence. On those rare occasions when his eyes met someone he knew, he'd just nod, yet still not say anything, not even hello.

David's desire to be a fireman may have derived in some measure from his attraction to uniforms—any kind of uniforms. He hung around the Co-op City firehouse and often tried out firemen's uniforms—even wore them home occasionally. His fascination for uniforms even led him to join the auxiliary police. That was in 1970 when he signed up with the unit at the 45th Precinct at 2877 Barkley Avenue in the Bronx. He served in that role for three years.

A psychologist, Salvatore Didato, who was called in to assist police in Westchester County after the Son of Sam case exploded in Yonkers, had a view on why David Berkowitz had leaned toward uniforms and why he joined the auxiliary police:

"Such desires play into his feeling of omnipotence, his grandiosity, his feelings of being above things.

"He would be a very thorough cop, if he ever were a cop. And as a fireman he probably would take chances that would be frowned on by the department. He would just sort of lose himself in his work."

Dr. Didato was by now aware of a second episode at Co-op City that involved David and another fire.

It had happened in late 1970. David was on the street and noticed smoke pouring from a twenty-sixth floor apartment window. The elevators weren't running, but David ran up the twenty-six flights, burst into the apartment and opened windows.

"This man wants power," Dr. Didato went on. "He's power-hungry. To be a policeman, to him means power. Putting out fires proves to him that he can control the forces of nature which go beyond human dimensions.

"Wrongdoing and fire give him an opportunity to show that he is powerful, but underneath all this power-striving is a very, very inadequate, weak individual..."

His fascination for uniforms continued into 1971. But now David Richard Berkowitz had been drawn to another style of uniform—the olive drab of Uncle Sam's Army...

CHAPTER XVIII

SAM IN UNCLE SAM'S ARMY

David Richard Berkowitz had one girl-friend in Co-op City who was closer to him than anyone—even his parents—had even been. She was pretty, slender Iris Gerhardt.

Iris was only fourteen years old when she first got to know Dave. He was sixteen and they went together for some fifteen months before Iris broke up with him.

"I was never intimate with him," Iris said recently after she had identified herself as David's onetime girlfriend and confidant. "It really wasn't like that between the two of us. I was only fourteen, although he might have wanted it that way."

"We just kissed each other on the lips in the building behind Co-op City when we all hung around in the local community club. But I must confess I liked him a lot."

Iris' concern for David was so great that her heart went out to him after he dropped out of high school at the end of his junior year to go into service.

The sadness, however, wasn't so much over his going into the Army but that his parents didn't think enough of him to at least see him off or give him a going-away present.

But there was a gift. David's stepsister, Julia's daughter, then living in the California commune, sent David a collage in the mail.

"It really got him mad," his friend said. "It was an anti-war type of thing with photographs and her own drawings that said American soldiers were killers and that Dave shouldn't do it, too. He really resented that. He showed it to us and said, 'How'd you like to get something like this if you were going into the Army?'"

Iris tried to lift David's spirits. She invited him to supper the night before he was to leave for induction, June 23, 1971.

"He looked like a whipped puppy," Iris recalled. "I got friends together and we had roast beef for dinner."

The next day she and some of the friends drove him to the Port Authority Bus Terminal in Manhattan to catch his ride to Fort Dix, New Jersey.

He remembered the farewell feast in one of his earliest letters to Iris:

"I must really thank you for the wonderful dinner you fed me. Since I am in the Army I have a strange feeling that I won't be getting delicious meals like that anymore."

In basic training, Berkowitz learned Army routine. He also learned about weaponry. On the rifle range he once scored thirty-seven bulls eyes—out of a hundred rounds fired. Not spectacular but perhaps of some comfort to America's safety if Berkowitz had been called upon to defend our shores. He fell in the middle range of the proficiency scale as an M-16 rifleman. He qualified as a sharpshooter.

Basic training also included messy details—like K.P. David pulled the nineteen-hour tours that were caught by every recruit. He had his turns at peeling potatoes, scrubbing pots, mopping floors, washing dishes, and everything else that goes with the job. He also caught guard duty, fire watch, barracks orderly, and more.

"I wish they'd let me sleep," he complained. "I never knew they had a hell above ground until I got to Fort Dix."

After his basic training was ended, he spent a brief furlough in New York and saw Iris Gerhardt. He then shipped out to Fort Polk, Louisiana, for advanced training. His intelligence scores and aptitude tests qualified him for schooling as a typist-clerk, although the basic preparation at Dix was as a light weapons infantryman.

On December 13th, 1971, he was sent to Korea and assigned to the 17th Infantry's 1st Battalion. It was in Korea where Berkowitz by all accounts, including his own vivid narratives in many letters home, had the drug experience on a scale so large that it effected dramatic changes in his personality and demeanor.

One of the earliest of these alterations was in his sudden shift from being a nominal right-winger when he entered service to a militant opponent of war and violence. He took up leftist causes. He wrote to friends in the Bronx to support the Students for a Democratic Society.

"Keep the movement moving on the home front and I'll keep it moving here," Berkowitz appealed in one letter.

His correspondence to friends and to Iris Gerhardt were slowly yet inevitably shaping a Dorian-like self-portrait, indeed an ever growing tapestry of his always-troubled mind's degeneration and the torment abuilding inside him.

Furthermore, to some observers those mutations showed the incubation of madness in David Berkowitz.

He had illusions and delusions, too.

David also had his doubts about whether he was born a Christian or a Jew. The fact that his natural father's name was Falco had never convinced David that he was born a Christian. At least not a whole one. For he often reasoned that his mother might have been a Jew. And why shouldn't she have been, he often asked? After all she gave him up for adoption to a Jewish couple, didn't she?

In Korea now, the metamorphosis went to another extreme. He began having conversations with Christ.

"One day me and Jesus talked ya know, the usual story," he wrote home. "Anyhow, we got to some big thinking. So I decided to do what I wanted to do in this particular situation. It worked perfect. They court-martialed me of course."

He was brought up on military charges for having refused to carry his rifle on a detail. He was busted from Specialist 4th Class to

Private 1st Class after his conviction.

The marijuana and LSD and other hard drugs David was taking in Korea were making him see changing colors—reds and blues and purples. He descended into a nebulous never-never land that caused him to be irrational and illogical in most conversations. Soldiers shunned him. They look upon him as some kind of a nut.

His duty in Korea ended thirteen months after he had arrived there, on January 4th, 1973. Until he received his orders to ship out, David Berkowitz had been deathly afraid that his new assignment would be Vietman—where they were shooting at each other with live ammunition. His new post, however, was back in the States—Fort Knox, Kentucky.

He began reading the Bible now. He called to task the soldiers who went to bars on weekends. He told them to stay out of such places. He was hawking religion all over the base. He tried to sell Jesus to Christians and non-Christians alike.

Davi Zammit who served with David Berkowitz at Fort Knox recalled:

"He was telling the guys they shouldn't be drinking and swearing and running around with women. But as an individual, I didn't think he was bad. He was a little off sometimes, but so were a few other guys who seemed just as strange."

Zammit said Berkowitz always had a neat appearance. He had his uniform pressed, shoes shined, and seemed to like things in their places, although he wasn't imbued with anything remotely resembling the West Point fervor for military perfection.

Yet it certainly was an improvement over the way he had kept his room at home.

They called him Berk or Berky, seldom David or Dave. He played first base on the baseball team of the 8th Training Brigade, 4th Battalion. Soldiers who remembered him there said he hit and fielded exceptionally well—as he had in his earlier years in the East Bronx.

But he never went with the fellows to the Knox Lounge where live bands entertained on weekends. He chose revival meetings instead.

So it was that he went for conversion from Judaism to Christianity on May 6, 1973, after attending services three times a week at the Beth Haven Baptist Church in Louisville.

Jim Almond, who was also stationed at the Army post, invited Berkowitz to church with him.

"I just asked him to go with me one day," Almond said in an interview at his home in Greenville, South Carolina.

"He said, 'I'm a Jew.'

"I told him I didn't care what he was, did he want to go to church?

"Well, we went and he really enjoyed it. He went forward at the invitation (to accept Christ as one's personal saviour from sin).

"And after the service, he came up to me grinning and laughing and saying, 'Man, I'm saved.'

"Then we came back that same day for the evening service and he went forward again at the invitation. He told me afterward that he just wanted to make sure it took."

Almond also remembered that Berkowitz had led an energetic Christian life for about a year at Fort Knox.

"But then he started backsliding just before his discharge. I heard Dave's parents practically disowned him after he became a Christian.

"He started hanging around with guys who drank and smoked pot and had dirty pictures on their walls. Maybe he was worried about going home and being lonely. Loneliness is a killer."

But before his release from service, David Berkowitz, Christian, made tremendous impressions on other people.

"He made a profession in Jesus Christ here," explained the Rev. Tom Wallace, Beth Haven's pastor. "I baptized the fellow. I noted he was a Jewish boy who had found Christ.

"Anytime a Jewish person comes forward to take a stand in a Baptist church, it's a little special. I asked the people to pray for him."

Some church members hadn't forgotten David Berkowitz as a soldier attending services, Sundays and evenings as well as mid-week prayer meeting.

Terri Luce, who was going on sixteen at the time, had a vivid recollection of Berkowitz. Terri served as a stewardess on one of the church buses which carried soldiers from Fort

Knox to the church.

"He was a really fantastic guy with a great personality," offered Miss Luce. "On the bus he would tell Bible stories to the kids. We talked all the time, mostly about church activities and spiritual things.

"He was in the Army and my dad was in the Army and we got along well. My parents really thought a lot of him."

Miss Luce's mother, Rosalie, said she also had a distinct remembrance of the man labelled Son of Sam, the .44-caliber killer.

"He was a great soul-winner. I never heard him say an unkind word. He brought a lot of GIs in from the base. It breaks my heart to see what happened now.

"I still don't believe it was him. But if it was, I'm just thankful he was saved. The Bible says, once saved, always saved..."

Back at the barracks and the realism of what was happening to him, David Berkowitz, the Christian, now tried to convert others, or at least lead them into the House of the Lord for worship. He told everyone they would be damned if they didn't accept Christ.

John Bartus was one of those he tried to shepherd to church.

"A couple of times he tried to give me the religious thing," Bartus said. "He tried to convince me that I should get back with Jesus. He tried it with a lot of the guys in the barracks.

"But he never got that far."

He also wrote poetry and read books such as

263

The Late Great Planet Earth, a 1973 religious tome by Hal Lindsey and C. C. Carlson.

His old friends were turned off by David's all-consuming involvement with the "Holy Rollers" and revival meetings he attended constantly. He was looked on as a Jesus freak and a deaf ear was turned to his self-righteous rantings about the evils of drinking and swearing and promiscuous sex.

On those rare occasions when he spoke lucidly about his experiences in Korea, he confided in friends that he had taken drugs because it was the thing to do, that everyone was taking them—everything from LSD and heroin and cocaine to uppers and downers.

He spoke somewhat shyly about his brief alleged encounters with Korean women, but never professed to have had sexual intercourse with any. He simply said in effect that they led him around, which wasn't saying much of anything about a relationship with the opposite sex. He never discussed the girls back home, not even Iris Gerhardt.

Another of his favorite topics of conversation was about getting a discharge as a conscientious objector. But he never went through with the filing of such a request.

He finally received his discharge on June 24, 1974—just three years and a day after he began active duty in Uncle Sam's Army. He was given a general discharge, according to records viewed at the Pentagon. He was also awarded two routine decorations for serving in Korea—the National Defense Service

Medal and the Armed Forces Expeditionary Medal. David Berkowitz had come out of the Army a bigger pussycat then what he was when he went in.

Who on earth could have predicted that this pacific young man, despite his many hangups and all his other idiosyncracies, could be moving toward a day when he would be accused of being the most hellish killer in all New York City's history?

CHAPTER XIX

LETTERS FROM A LOVER

Her voice was tremulous and she was concerned about her own good reputation, which she felt had to be protected. For Iris Gerhardt was married now and as Mrs. Cary Klausner was more than eight months pregnant. She didn't want her neighbors in Westland, the Detroit suburb, to misunderstand about her relationship with David Richard Berkowitz.

But then, too, the *New York News* and *New York Post* were hot for her letters from Dave and the $200 and $500 the two generous big city newspapers were paying respectively could help the family finances at a time like that.

Iris was only fourteen years old when she got to know Dave and barely sixteen when she broke with him "because I wanted to see other guys." But Mrs. Klausner said she and David continued to be "close friends."

So when he went into the Army in 1971, he immediately began writing to Iris Gerhardt. His letters, which Mrs. Klausner had saved, shape an amazing diary of a young soldier whose mind, boggled by the drugs and a detested order to carry a rifle, helped him on a trip that could truly be entitled *From Here To Insanity*.

In the beginning, the letters were gems of

innocence. As for example the first one, mailed July 8, 1971, from Fort Dix, where he was taking basic training as a private.

"I have been at Fort Dix for over fifteen days. Basic training is sure hard. I have to run 5 miles everyday. Getting up at 4:30 in the morning isn't easy...

"I am not really unhappy at all that I enlisted. Even though this life is very hard, I felt I just had to go. I always wanted to be on my own. I wanted to take up some responsibilities. There was nothing for me to do back home anyhow. There is one thing I miss, that's my friends... You had better write soon.

The next letter, written August 5th, has an ever-so-slightly disturbing reference to a gun, yet it's obviously written in jest:

"...you can see that I put in many hours of hard labor. I guess it's the price of wanting to serve my country...I had nothing to lose coming here. I should be home next week on a pass. I hope to see you.

"I haven't changed much except I lost 25 pounds. Better not get me mad because I'm good with a gun! Don't make me use it on you... Love, Dave."

After David Berkowitz finished his training at Dix, he came home on furlough and met Iris

Gerhardt briefly. They spoke. She didn't notice any appreciable change in the young man she knew—except that he had lost weight and looked trim.

Then he was off to Fort Polk for advanced training, followed by duty in Korea. It was there that he seemed to transform into a person whom Iris Gerhardt began not to understand at all. Even Berkowitz himself acknowledged a metamorphosis was coming over him.

A private first class in Infantry Company B, David wrote on January 21, 1972, and very quickly remembered Iris' birthday:

"Happy sweet sixteen . . . Did you know that I was in a down mood when I got your letter, then I read your letter and it totally paralyzed my mind. I think it's my fault that our going together never worked out. I never put any effort into our relationship. So don't apologize because you have nothing to worry about.

"I'll tell you what when I come home in June. I'll promise to make love to you all weekend long, okay? Will do it for old times sake.

"My mind has completely blew out. I have changed. You will probably be disappointed not to see the same old Dave anymore.

"I don't play anymore conservative patriot scenes.

"I woke up. The world is all fucked up

(thanks Nixon). We've got to have some peace.

"The only thing on my mind is Drugs, Music, Pollution, Poverty, Peace and Love.

"I really got into drugs ya know. It's different, kind of messed up. I guess I'm all fucked up but its part of life.

"I despise religion, hate prejustice (sic) greed, etc. That's all the world is. A cold mass of hell. It sucks.

"We're all doomed to the grave. When you think of death do you lose your breath or do you keep your cool?

"Listen love, think of God, it's the only way. I can't live in a world of atomic fear. I think there is some love left in the world.

"Oh...man, I'm all fucked up. Please straighten me out, please. I love you. Dave."

David Berkowitz who, as Mrs. Klausner recalled had always been a "sort of very unnoticeable young man...a guy you never would notice," now in Korea suddenly acquired a belligerence totally alien to his personality. A letter of February 2nd shows the change as he talks about refusing to carry a rifle:

"I'm glad your happy about getting my picture. It's not a joke picture, that's the way I always am. Hey, you must be getting mad at me for writing all these unhappy letters. Well, I guess I shouldn't sound so down all the time, but I can't help it. The fact is, I am feeling down, all the time.

"I suppose Ed (his closest friend) is doing okay in the Coast Guard. But you have to realize that the Army and the Coast Guard are two different services.

"Hey, guess what? They might transfer me to another unit. I'll either be a fire fighter, medic, ecologist, or game warden. I have finally proven to them that I'm not going to play with there (sic) guns anymore. I made myself promise that I was not to carry any weapons while my unit was on the field. So that day while I was in the chow line, a major and a captain walked up to me and said, 'Private, where is your gun?' And I said, I didn't bring it to the field and I refuse to bring it to the field.

"Well, all hell broke out after that. They just can't tell me when to carry a gun. I explained to them but they didn't do much good. I also explained it to the chaplain. And guess what? He's with me all the way. He never carried a gun in his life. He is trully (sic) a man of God, and so am I and he knows it.

"Of course, I'm for a court martial but I'll win. I'll have to prove that I'm a conscientious objector, which I am.

"It's going to be a ruff fight but I have one thing going for me. That is God. He's on my side.

"There is one thing you must admit about me. That is, when have you ever known me to say things about love, Peace, God, etc. I mean, can you ever remember me talking about all this back in the world...

"These feelings have been deep inside...now don't think I'm going insane or anything like that because I'm not ...yes it's the real me...they come out with a little help from my friends. I must truly thank my friends for helping me. Because now I'm an individual again. Free from the war pigs and there (sic) evil ways. I wouldn't want you to meet my friends. There (sic) not very nice..."

Disturbed by the change in him, Iris penned words of comfort and pleaded with David to keep himself in line. On February 21st, he responded:

"I like what you said in your letters. I guess I'll straighten out eventually.

"The following...are in my very own writings about today's society. I hope you will not be displeased with me for what I wrote. This is what's been on my mind. I've always had a guilty feeling about the stand I took when I was back home.

"You will note that I have gone one extreme to another. That's because I am finally facing reality.

"I am writing you with the hope you will understand ... I hope you will express your feelings truthfully. One thing I admire is a trully(sic) honest person. I hope you make out okay in school. Don't sweat it.

"I hated school too. Now I hate the Army more. I guess I'll have to suffer until I get out ... I'm looking forward to seeing the world again.

"Take care, love Dave."

Iris Gerhardt now sensed something else in David. As he sank more deeply into a morass of inability to cope with military life, he wrote more frequently. His next letter, on March 1st, virtually repeated an earlier one about his military trial.

"My court martial is coming up in a few weeks ... I have a good chance of winning according to the facts and review. There's a good chance that I'll be fined $50.00. If I win I can tell them to get fucked and I'll be transferred to another job which does not involve handling guns and ammunition.

"The reason I got court martialed was because I failed to obey a direct order from my company commander ... the C.O. noticed that I didn't have any weapons. When he asked me where my weapons were I told him very politely I didn't bring them and I went into telling him how I felt about carrying and using weapons. I said,

'Sir, I politely refuse to carry them because of my moral beliefs...'

"Well, he got kind of pissed off... He is a true lifer (career soldier), who dedicated his mind and body to the Army. So it's obvious I cannot talk to him about the peace movement. The only thing I'm worried about is my jurors. There (sic) all lifers too. They only think Army and kill the enemy...

"I'll beat these lifers ... keep straight... I guess you get a chance to see all my friends so say hello. They probably won't remember me. If you see Ed call him a war pig and a rightist militant... if he hits you let me know. Then I'll take care of him myself...

"I can't wait until tomorrow, it's pay day. I'll have to go and get some heavy acid and morphine so I can last out the month.

"Wish me luck.

"Love, Dave."

That letter was decorated with a series of small cartoons. One said "Smog Kills Kids." Other writings were, "Love Shall Dominate," "Hawks Vs Doves," "Pleasure," "Ecology for Survival," "Peace Means," "Love Is?" "Death Is?" He wrote another letter two weeks later in which he apologized for keeping Iris Gerhardt waiting. Mrs. Klausner explained:

"I kept answering those letters as fast as I got them. I hoped it would keep him together.

He seemed a different David to the one I knew."

There was no leveling off of his revulsion for authority and discipline in the letter of March 14th:

"I'm sorry you had to wait awhile for this letter but it was hard to start.

"I could ask you how things are back in the world but I know you are making it okay...

"Do you know what the lifers made me do? They made me take a haircut. Man am I pissed off. Just because they love crewcuts, they gotta try to chop my head up...

"I'm still trying to find a way to go straight. It's not easy to find a way so I'm still searching.

"Leave it up to the fucked up Army. They postponed my court martial a week. I can't wait to get it over with...

"So far from reading this you would think I'm getting by okay. Well, I'm not. I've got some bad news for you. You know how the Army messes and changes things around the last minute... My original mid-term leave was for June. They had nothing better to do so they moved them back to late August or September...

"I feel pretty bad now because I really wanted to get back to see you...

"I had my hopes up so much... I'll have to write you another letter real soon. I happen to be speechless right now.

"Love, Dave."

His desperation increased and four days after the last letter, on March 18th, he scribbled another to Iris:

"Boy, love, you know I'm really down. I was just waiting and waiting to go home.

"Since I got here all I've been doing is fighting the establishment. It gets pretty hard to keep fighting all the time but I and a few others know where (sic) right.

"I'm just to (sic) anxious to see this great new world develop. But I get down sometimes when I see and think that I'll be dead before I can ever see this change take place. I don't feel like fighting. When I say fighting I don't mean with any violence. When do you think people will see the light...

"It gets really bad when I get the impression that I have no support from anybody and I'm fighting a losing battle. I often feel this way so I get the urge to escape for awhile. In other words I just take my mind out of the rat race and get into deep meditation. When I do it gives me a chance to think and plan my next move.

"However lately I found I have been escaping quite often and I got in quite a mess. The wierd thing is I sometimes like the mess I'm in...

"Do you think you really know what love is? I was looking forward to heading back home. It would of given me a chance to rest my mind a bit before it busts open...

"I just might turn out to be one of those unhappy citizens who gave up fighting a long time ago and just fell helplessly into the usual rat race. Sometimes I feel that the only time peace will come is when I'm dead...

"Or I might turn out to be a lifetime freak...

"I will write you soon because I love you...

"Love, Dave."

David Berkowitz, who disdained bars and discos at home, often took Iris Gerhardt to task for going to such teenage gathering places as George's, a lounge, and the Lollipop, a disco, both in New Rochelle. "What are you doing that for?" he would demand, his voice sarcastic, abrasive. "You shouldn't be going out to those places. Come to my digs and listen to the stereo..."

But Iris said she never did.

In Korea now, David, the non-drinker, was beginning to get much more deeply into drugs. Iris had written him two letters before he sent this one on April 8th:

"I really dig love & peace...Do you know what? I feel just like a useless expendible machine. That's right when I look in the mirror all I see is one green soldier looking back at me. I feel like a robot being told when and where I can do things. I wish I could get a bike and travel around the open plains of the land.

"Say, how is Oscar the owl? (Iris' pet bird). I remember that old fat fellow. I'm getting jealous of him. I don't want him to stay in your bedroom...I'd rather be there myself...

"How is America? Do you know that for the last few days, I've been so doped up that I feel I'm on a flying carpet. Wow, what a head. Well at least time floats by. I wish I could move the clock forward...

"Guess what? I've come across an amazing discovery...I have finally made a conclusion. That is, God is real. Believe me, he's as you and me. I can't begin to tell you about it. Imagine if there were no countries to fight and die for. Imagine if man had no religion. I'm not the only dreamer.

"Love ya, Dave."

Iris warned David again about the danger of taking drugs as she had often done. David acknowledged that latest admonition in his April 22nd missive:

"I know that I haven't wrote for awhile. My court martial was put off...

"I'm sure you know what's going on in Vietnam...Our officers would sure like us to go. We all think they are insane...since we're on standby for 'Nam and figuring the war won't be over until the year 2001, you can assume I won't be home for awhile...

"Let us drink a toast to the government for there (sic) very cool ingenuity in getting us back in 'Nam...

"Oh by the way. Don't worry about me killing myself on drugs. I've got too much to do in life to sky out to (sic) soon. I'll be around for awhile.

"Hey do you know that I miss you? I really do...

"So hang in there.

"Blessed are the Peacemakers. For they are the children of God.

"Love, Dave."

Many of his letters were cluttered with misspellings and clumsy sentences, a sign of his inadequate formal education. But his messages were always clear and readily understandable.

In his next letter thirteen days later, Berkowitz, raised in the Jewish faith, talked about Jesus Christ—that was still many months before his conversion to Christianity. In the letter he also addressed himself to the future—to the day when he returned from service a changed person. The date was May 5th and the letter read:

"Jesus Christ fought real hard and he never lived to see the changes. They haven't come so he's still waiting... I've committed my body to an evil organiza-

278

tion. I think it's time to uncommit myself...

"I have much hope and faith in God and Peace. I have much love for people like you. I don't want to learn how to kill my fellow man...

"There ain't nobody gonna get rich over my dead body. Nobody is gonna send me to a war so they can make some money by having me use their products like guns, bullets, bombs, etc.

"When I get back you will see a new Dave.

"The Army doesn't like the changes that came over me so they try to break me. The Army reminds me of a baby. If a toy works, he throws it on the floor and drops it in the bottom of his toy chest.

"So until I get my head together, I'll be thinking of some solutions...

"Remember I love you! Dave."

As Mrs. Klausner looked back on that period, she remembered the feeling "he would do something crazy. I didn't know what, but he was really asking over and over again for help." He was certainly crying out for freedom when he wrote to Iris on June 7th:

"...As far as the Army goes it's just one big bummer. We (me and the Army) don't get along too well...I think it's because I see the Army as nothing more than a tool of the government to use against another nation. It's just a game of politics.

"I cannot see why man would wage war on another man. We're all supposed to love each other but we don't...

"I want to promote love and brotherhood. We don't have much love here on earth... War never did a person any good...

"I want to be free... I will be pretty soon. There is something I must do first. Give me about 50 days for planning...

"I sure would like mankind to be free. Hey love, tell me how to be free, tell me how to find peace. I haven't found any answers yet. Can you think of some?

"Love ya always, Dave."

When Iris Gerhardt received David Berkowitz's next letter, written August 14, 1972, she finally felt that he had "flipped out" and needed help. He now seemed to be possessed by demonic ideas:

"They taught me how to fight. They taught me about many weapons, demolition, riot control and self defense.

"All of these courses will come in handy one day. I plan to use them and it's not going to be the way the lifers (the career Army men he often referred to) want me to use them. I will use these tactics to destroy them the way they destroyed millions of people through the wars they started. One day there will be a better world.

"After a few heads from the heads of state are removed...the poor man is not lazy like the rich man...I am displeased with it and I will try to change it...I will make it my resolution to find out what is in the heads of our fearless leaders. I will find out what is in their heads even if I have to crack them wide open...I hate rebels but I love revolutionaries.

"Love ya always, Dave."

All David Berkowitz's letters were kept by Iris Gerhardt. She wasn't quite certain as to why she held onto them, but now they remain in her possession for a good reason.

"They are a sad reminder of a strange relationship, a friendship that had meaning to me..."

She saw David twice after he came out of the Army. One of those times they had a snowball fight outside Bronx Community College which both had attended for a while at different times.

"He seemed much more grown up and mature, but there was a change. Then I saw him once again and I knew he needed help. But there was little I could do."

Mrs. Klausner's husband, a young executive with a New York based firm, wanted to know why Iris hadn't tried to steer Berkowitz to a psychiatrist when she saw through the letters that he was "crazy, going over the wall?"

With a shrug, Mrs. Klausner replied:

"I just thought he wasn't a violent person. He never got into fights. I only saw him angry once. He had an argument with his friend Eddie. And he just said, 'I'm not talking to Eddie for a while.' He never talked badly about anyone..."

Klausner, who also knew Berkowitz to say hello to, had an attitude of his own toward the man exposed as Son of Sam, the .44-caliber killer:

"I don't think about him. I think about the victims. If he came through this door right now I would blow him away with my shotgun and pull his body inside and say he tried to break in."

Mrs. Klausner shook her head.

"I know it's wrong but I still have this feeling for this poor lonely guy. I just feel so sorry for him..."

CHAPTER XX

HIS DOUBLE LIFE—ECHOES
OF JEKYLL AND HYDE

Despite the drugs and all other disturbing distractions during those three years in the Army, David Berkowitz returned to his parents apartment in the Bronx exhibiting the promise of leading a more serene and fruitful life.

But no sooner had he come home than the stability of family life that he yearned for so long was taken away suddenly. His father and mother had finalized their plans to live Nat's retirement in a Florida condominium complex called Regal Gardens in Boynton.

They were going to move just as soon as they could sell their four-and-a-half room Co-op City apartment.

It was six months more, however, before Nat and Julia moved out, because it took that long to find a buyer.

Meanwhile, the father watched with increasing anxiety his son's obsession with religion. It was bad enough, Nat Berkowitz felt, that David wouldn't finish high school and go to college. But to be on a Jesus freak kick, this boy who had been Bar Mitzvahed, was intolerable to the father.

"Stop, please stop this business about Christ," Nat pleaded. "I can't stand to listen to you. Who do you think you are, a priest? Stop it."

His new beliefs also disenfranchised David from most of his friends, those from the old neighborhood, those he mingled with in the Summer at the Shorehaven Beach Club in Classon Point, and the ones in Co-op City.

"At least if you don't go to college, get a job, David," his father begged.

Finally David found employment. It was as a guard for IBI Security Company of Jamaica, Queens. He was assigned to work the loading docks and prevent thefts at the Universal Car Loading Company at 351 Tenth Avenue on Manhattan's West Side.

He performed with excellence on the job. He was required to patrol with a vicious German shepherd guard dog. Some other guards for IBI were terrified of the dogs—they feared they'd turn against them. Before he landed that job, David Berkowitz had filled an interim period as an itinerant cab driver.

As the year end approached, David Berkowitz went apartment hunting. Nat and Pearl had found a buyer for their place. He was Paul Meinhofer, then a 23-year-old assistant traffic manager of the Eagle Electric Company.

Meinhofer never saw David on the two visits he and his wife paid to the Berkowitzes' apartment before signing the agreement of sale.

"On our first visit when we went to see what the apartment was like," Meinhofer said, "we didn't get into the second bedroom. Mr.

Berkowitz told us, 'My son is in there. I responded, 'O.K., fine, don't disturb him. I have an idea what the room is like. We'll look in the next time.'"

When the Meinhofers visited the apartment again the bedroom was empty.

"Nowadays," Meinhofer said recently, "our cat sleeps in there."

David had found a one-bedroom apartment at 2161 Barnes Avenue in the Bronx—where he soon encountered the annoyance of the hard-of-hearing woman who played her TV too loud. The rent was $130 a month and his parents helped out by giving David some furniture, including the pieces in his own room to take to his new living quarters.

Though he was doing well as a guard, David felt he should be in something more productive. His late adoptive mother Pearl's brother had been looking long and hard for a better job for David.

Meanwhile, however, David had decided to follow his father's advice and try to get an education. So David registered at Bronx Community College in February, 1975.

He attended on a regular basis and, according to the school's records, he had a 2.89, or high C, average. He had earned thirty-seven credits by the time he ran afoul of the law.

David managed to combine school and work and when his uncle finally found him a better job he took it.

That was in July, 1976, during the Summer

recess at the two-year college. David went into his uncle's line of work—the sheet-metal business. The job was with the Wolf and Munier Company in Elmsford, Westchester County. His job entailed loading and unloading trucks. He was paid $5 an hour for a 35-hour week—$175 before taxes, social security, and the rest of the deductions, which in this case also involved dues to the sheet-metal workers union.

July of 1976 was the month he started as a sheet metal worker. It was the same month that Donna Lauria was killed and Jody Valente was wounded by the .44-caliber killer in his first foray.

What clue can we trawl from David Richard Berkowitz's activities then to betray him as the man police were to charge was the Son of Sam, the .44-caliber killer?

He displayed no sign of violence or hatred against anyone. Unless you can consider a peaceful union demonstration a clue in the triggering of such bizarre and violent behavior.

David Berkowitz took part in a peaceful protest against demolition of the White Plains Courthouse in the county seat of Westchester. While there with other sheet-metal workers, he sold one of them his tools—a hammer, a screwdriver, and vise grips. It was lunchtime and Berkowitz left. He never came back to his job.

By February of 1977, just days after Christine Freund was murdered in Queens,

David Richard Berkowitz walked into the Bronx General Post Office on the Grand Concourse at 149th Street and applied for a job.

By now he was no longer living on Barnes Avenue. He had since the previous February moved out, gone to stay three months at Jack and Nann Cassara's house in New Rochelle, then moved into the apartment in Yonkers.

Postmaster Frank Viola at the Bronx GPO recalled the job interview with David Berkowitz.

"After he took the test for the job and scored 85.5 per cent, which included a 5 per cent credit for being a veteran, he came in for the interview. Unlike some of the others, he had a clean appearance and spoke well."

Berkowitz was hired as a part-time postal employee and assigned to be a ZMT operator—a sort of mail sorter feeding the noisy machine sixty envelopes per minute.

He earned $7 an hour and went on the 4 p.m. to 12:30 a.m. shift.

At the Post Office the talk was constantly about the .44-caliber killer. For by the time David Berkowitz came to work there, the psychopathic gunman had claimed his third murder victim, Virginia Voskerichian.

No one in wildest flight of fancy at the Post Office could have imagined that the pleasant young man with the plain face and quiet, subdued personality could have been the dreaded gunman.

Least of all Theresa Graziano, who went

through training for the job with David and worked alongside him in the GPO. She even lunched frequently with him in the cafeteria.

"He talked like anyone else," she said. "There was no conversation with him about the .44-caliber killer although I was terrified of him."

She took a deep breath.

"To think how afraid I was all those months—and then to be told I was working next to the man I was so afraid of all that time!"

George Moffa, a 23-year-old co-worker at the GPO, recalled having had some talk with Berkowitz about Son of Sam.

"I'd sit in the cafeteria having coffee with him and say how I'd like to get my hands on that guy and kill him," said Moffa who knew three of the victims—the Bronx girls, Donna Lauria, Jody Valente, and Valentina Suriani.

"Dave would just sit there and agree with everything I said. He would say, 'Yeah, they gotta get that guy. He's really doing bad things and should be caught.'"

The last time Moffa saw Berkowitz was on Wednesday, July 27—four days before the .44-caliber killer struck for the final time. Berkowitz had worked his last day on Friday, July 29th—the anniversary date when the entire NYPD had waited for him to strike.

But the .44-caliber killer didn't hit again until two days later, July 31st. That was when he fatally wounded Stacy Moskowitz and blinded Robert Violante in the stunning attack in Brooklyn.

The next afternoon, David Berkowitz failed to show up for work. He never returned to the GPO.

Meanwhile, Berkowitz's problems with the hard-of-hearing woman, with the Cassaras, and with Sam Carr were being followed up with a more serious run-in with one of his downstairs tenants at 35 Pine Street in Yonkers.

The downstairs neighbor was Craig Glassman, a 29-year-old Westchester County deputy sheriff. He lived in Apartment 6-E, directly beneath Berkowitz's 7-E. Since the beginning of June, Glassman had been bombarded with threatening messages.

Glassman had no idea who was harrassing him. But he thought the time had damn well come to find out. For on Saturday, August 6th a fire broke out at the base of his apartment door. In the burning pile of rubbish the arsonist had also tossed a handful of .22-caliber bullets. But the fire was doused before it spread too far, although it caused considerable damage to Glassman's apartment. The bullets didn't explode.

After the fire, Glassman began suspecting his upstairs neighbor, Berkowitz. He confided his suspicion in his boss, Sheriff Thomas Delaney, as well as police and fire officials.

But—as it had been in the complaint from Jack Cassara—Craig Glassman's finger of accusation pointed at Berkowitz was based only on suspicion, nothing solid enough to warrant arrest.

The notes sent to him had no rhyme nor did they pinpoint a particular grievance, which made it so difficult for Glassman to suspect anyone for all those months.

"You will be punished," read one note. "How dare you force me into the night to do your bidding. True, I am the killer, but Craig the killer kills on your command. The streets have been filled with blood at the request of Craig."

It was signed, "Your brother."

Another letter said:

"Cruel, crazy Craig, the streets will run with your blood in your honor."

Glassman had never knowingly seen Berkowitz during the time the notes were being sent to him.

"I didn't know him at all, had no idea he lived upstairs. But I guess he knew who I was and had seen me in uniform coming into and leaving the building."

It was after the fire and his report to Yonkers police that he learned about others in Westchester—namely his neighbor Sam Carr and the Cassaras in New Rochelle—having received similar crazy notes.

That's when David Berkowitz suddenly loomed as the suspect.

Looking back on those notes and the message they conveyed, Glassman remained totally mystified about what prompted Berkowitz to take a dislike to him.

"Who knows what triggered him. Who

knows what crazy thoughts went through his mind?"

Who indeed knows...?

Perhaps if we could go back to another era and ask Robert Louis Stevenson for some views, we might have an answer. For *Dr. Jekyll and Mr. Hyde* certainly seem to figure somewhere in the case of Son of Sam, the .44-caliber killer...

AFTER THE FACT

BOOK THREE

CHAPTER XXI

"I WAS COMMANDED TO KILL..."

His digs were a scene out of skid row.

David Berkowitz had a view of the Hudson River and the beautiful grim, gray New Jersey Palisades from his apartment window. Yet he chose to hang sheets over the windows which obliterated the scene.

Obviously he hadn't tried curtains.

The squalor of the apartment was appalling. Graffiti on the walls was overwhelming.

"Hi
"My name is
"Mr. Williams
"And I live
"In this hole"

Then an arrow pointed to a hole to the left of the message. The hole had been punched—or hammered—into the plasterboard wall.

Shades of the opening in Mrs. Shirley Schilkraut's Co-op City apartment wall to put out her Heinz baked beans "fire"?

"I have several
"Children who I'm turning
"Into killers. Wait
"Till they grow up."

To the right of the block-letter writing was the windup of the message that was spelled out aside the hole:

"My Neighbors
"I have no respect
"For and I treat them
"Like shit.
            "Sincerely
            "Williams"

Another scribbled message asserted, "God saves us from Craig Glassman," the downstairs neighbor who had been the target of venemous and threatening letters and whose apartment was damaged by fire.

Pornographic magazines were scattered near the bed which was a roaring, disorderly mess of rumpled sheets and comforters.

The floor was cluttered with other books—a test manual for postal carriers, another test text for bus drivers, volumes such as *Geology Made Simple* and an Army publication called *Survival, Evasion and Escape.*

Several phonograph records—mostly love themes—were piled incongruously, messily on the floor.

Back at police headquarters, detectives closeted with the suspect cascaded questions at him in an endless torrent.

"From the beginning all I wanted was ten minutes with him in a motel room so I could find out about the guy I had been hunting for six months," said Detective Gerald Shevlin.

Shevlin was one of ten detectives from Inspector Timothy Dowd's task force who'd been given free reign to pump the suspect. His constitutional rights had been read to David Richard Berkowitz, but that was a mere formality. Everybody whoever sat on the U.S. Supreme Court from Oliver Wendell Holmes to Benjamin Nathan Cardozo to Warren Burger, knew the cops were never about to give this poor Jewish boy from the Bronx half a chance to call himself a lawyer before those sleuths from Dowd's team had grilled him bone dry.

"Why, why, did you kill them?" one detective demanded in Room 1312, which was Chief of Detectives Keenan's office.

"It was a command," the beleaguered suspect answered. "I had a sign and I followed it. Sam told me what to do and I did it..."

"Who is Sam?" another officer wanted to know.

"His commands came to me through his dog. They told me to kill. Sam is the devil."

When asked whether Sam was the man named Carr who's dog had been shot, Berkowitz smiled wanly. "What do you think?" he prodded his questioners.

Get off the Sam Carr kick. That's a Yonkers police case. Ask him about the killings. Get evidence—a confession that will stand up in court—that he's the .44-caliber killer. That gun you found in his car. The real killer could have thrown it there. Berkowitz wouldn't even need a smart lawyer to put that point over in court.

"Did you ever write to Captain Borrelli?"

"Jesus, yes. Are you stupid. Didn't you read the newspapers...?"

Nothing had ever been published anywhere about the message in that note. Only the one to Jimmy Breslin had been revealed.

"Remember what you said, Dave?"

"Like what?"

"What you liked about Queens in particular."

"Oh, shit, yeah. I said that the girls in Queens are prettier."

"How'd you sign the letter?"

"The Monster."

"Did you call yourself anything else that you remember?"

"The Chubby Behemoth..."

Many hours later Inspector Dowd was to say triumphantly:

"It's only because we knew tonight would come that we didn't release that letter to the press. What he's revealed to us in his statement can leave no doubt that he wrote it. Only he would have known the key identities and statements in that letter."

The elusive fugitive who had been so long the terror of the town wasn't going to be let off the hook after that much of a confession. His questioners wanted chapter and verse on the murders. Too, they wanted to learn from the killer—if indeed he was the killer—what his

298

pattern was. They wanted to know that so they could be guided in the future if ever another such madman should visit the city.

"Sure I was out almost every night, driving, looking for game," Berkowitz replied to a question. "Ever since last year, since Donna Lauria I would look and wait for a sign from Sam. I'd look for a parking space for my car. If I found one right away I'd know I was being commanded. Then I'd hit 'em."

Why did he single out Miss Lauria for special remembrance when he wrote to Breslin. Did she have any deeper meaning to him than other victims?

"She was a nice girl...No, I didn't know her...I just could tell she was nice...You know something...I even went to St. Raymond's Cemetery to visit her grave. But it was a bitch to find. I just gave it up..."

Was he actually attracted to girls with long, dark hair?

That question was one of the few during the long hours of interrogation that provoked laughter in the suspect. He was, in fact, almost disparaging of the police, the psychologists and psychiatrists, and others who speculated on his modus operandi and motivations.

"Hair had nothing to do with what I did. And I didn't wear a wig ever...I never had any hangups on sex. I'm the kind of guy who went out with a broad would get in the first time—or I quit her."

The girls in Queens that he mentioned in

his letter to Captain Borelli?

"Yeah, they're the best fuckin' I guess. But I don't want you to quote me because I don't want to hurt any girls' feelings in the Bronx either."

Speaking in short, clipped sentences, clearly and lucidly, David Berkowitz filled his interrogators' appetites for every detail about his thirteen-month orgy of murder and maiming.

He revealed that he was captured just in the nick of time last night—because when the cops grabbed him...

"I was gonna drive you guys out of your bird. I was heading for Riverdale jn the Bronx. I was gonna look for a sign there tonight."

There was a note in his car, addressed to the Suffolk County Police, warning that he would strike there. What was that about?

"I had driven out to Westhampton Beach last week. I was looking for a sign but I didn't get none. So I went home."

Another time recently, Berkowitz claimed he'd roamed the Huntington area of Suffolk County but again got no directive from Sam— or the dog.

He was asked whether he remembered Mrs. Davis, who spotted him on the street after the shooting in Bensonhurst.

"The woman with the dog? Yeah, she kinda threw me off for a minute. I saw her there and I didn't want her to take too much notice of me. So I turned off the street as fast as I could."

He revealed that he had been to the

playground earlier, that he had been sitting on a swing and been lining up a couple in a blue car for a hit. But the couple, parked under the bright sodium-vapor lamp, then shifted the car's position and went into the darkness.

"Then when the other car came in, I got the sign and I shot them."

The couple in the darkness were Tommy Z and his girlfriend. It was Tommy who saw the shooting of Stacy Moskowitz and Robert Violante through his rear view mirror.

The pattern changed just once in the eight attacks Son of Sam committed. Virginia Voskerichian was alone whereas all the other victims were with someone else. Why did he shoot the Columbia coed that night?

"It was commanded that I shoot her."

The suspect also shot some holes into other theories that investigators had developed about the killer's pattern of attack.

Berkowitz said he didn't always fire from the combat-style two-handed position; he never went to a discotheque or public place to seek out a victim; he didn't always save the fifth or last bullet for himself or to fight off capture.

"I shot off five rounds twice, but you just didn't find the fifth slugs."

Where did he get the .44?

"An Army buddy in Texas bought it down there for me a couple years ago."

What was the submachine gun doing in his car, his interrogators wanted to know after the wearying hours of questioning drew to a windup.

"I was looking to tangle assholes with some cops, that's why I had it with me. "I wanted to get into a shootout. I wanted to get killed, but I wanted to take some cops with me."

David Richard Berkowitz had fulfilled some chilling predictions in his letters from Korea.

"...I might turn out to be a lifetime freak...They taught me about many weapons...I will use these tactics to destroy..."

And now, less than twenty-four hours after his spectacular arrest, he had also attained the sort of notoriety that for most of his twenty-four years he never dreamed could come to him. For there it was in the lead headline of the *New York Times*:

BERKOWITZ HEAVILY GUARDED,
    ARRAIGNED AND HELD FOR TESTING

It wasn't:

CARTER, HEAVILY GUARDED,
     ON TRIP TO MIDDLE EAST

Nor:

BEAME, HEAVILY GUARDED,
    AFTER COLUMN BY BRESLIN

No. It was:

BERKOWITZ HEAVILY GUARDED,
    ARRAIGNED AND HELD FOR TESTING

Richard David Berkowitz, who went to P.S. 57 in the Bronx, who had his ear pulled by Miss Drucker in the third grade, had been Bar Mitzvahed in Adah Israel Temple, called a "Jewboy" and taunted about his adoption, who hung his step-sister's impressionistic painting upside down, who kissed Iris Gerhardt behind the building in Co-op City, who went into the Army wanting to save the country and came out wanting to destroy it, who was saved by Jesus, this schmuck as he was known in the parlance of his old East Bronx neighborhood—had finally and at long last made it to the top of the world, in the *New York Times*, no less.

David Richard Berkowitz—a household name!

"How totally and mundane, how ordinary, that a parking ticket should lead to this happy ending," remarked Police Commissioner Codd.

It's puzzling that Codd should have been so surprised. Hadn't he heard what Inspector Levitan said during Stacy Moskowitz's funeral? "It'll probably be some silly traffic violation. They'll bring him in for investigation and it'll turn out to be him."

Guarded by a veritable army of police officers, detectives, correction officers and everybody else who could get into the act, David Richard Berkowitz was arraigned later that Thursday morning of August 11 in

Brooklyn Criminal Court before Acting Supreme Court Justice Richard A. Brown.

"You, sir, are David Berkowitz?" Justice Brown asked firmly.

"Yes, sir," Berkowitz snapped.

That's all the most notorious suspect in all New York history had to say during the fifteen minute proceedings.

Berkowitz stood unmoving, hands handcuffed behind his back, as the judge read the charges: second-degree murder for the killing of Stacy Moskowitz, second-degree assault for the shooting of Robert Violante.

"The position of the people," said Assistant District Attorney Ronald Aiello "is that your honor does have before him the .44-caliber killer also known as Son of Sam. And the position of the district attorney is that he should be held without bail."

As if Brown was about to let David Berkowitz walk out of the courtroom, angry crowds gathered in the street outside the courthouse, with many shouting, "Kill him! Kill him! The last thing in the world that His Honor would have done was consider anything but tossing Berkowitz into the slammer and throwing the key away.

Even David's lawyers who had mysteriously materialized from nowhere to represent him agreed with the court. Actually, Mark J. Heller, who hailed from Mineola in Nassau County, had been retained by the suspect's father, who had flown up from his retirement home in Florida to offer what help he could to

David.

Heller and two associates, Leon Stern and Ira Jultak, were in court to represent young Berkowitz. But the talking was done before the bench by a mouthpiece who went by the name of Philip Peltz. How he got into the act, Judge Brown didn't ask. But His Honor listened to Peltz say:

"If it pleases the court, it will certainly be in the best interest of the defendant that he not be at liberty at this time."

What Peltz should have said was, I really want to get this guy in the can because I figure to make a big bundle on him . . . Wow, what a hell of a gold mine he can be—books, magazines, TV, movies, foreign sales. Maybe if I play my hand right I can team up with Breslin and we could go on the road as an act. Who knows, they might even invite me on the Today Show!

As it turned out, David Berkowitz was committed by Judge Brown to the Psychiatric Division of Kings County Hospital for a determination of his capacity to understand the charges against him.

There was irony in that commitment, for the man the accused killer had blinded, Robert Violante, was in the very same hospital at that precise point in time—and still uncertain whether he'd ever see through his severely damaged right eye.

Meanwhile, Phil Peltz made tracks to the psychiatric cell where Dave Berkowitz was holed up. Peltz toted a tape recorder and obviously had the prisoner spill his guts out about the crimes he allegedly committed and anything else that the interviewer could get the interviewee to say.

Then Peltz very cagily gave a flunky the mission of going to the News and offering the tapes for $50,000. The News turned the offer down. Not because it was being limited to only "North American Sunday rights," but because the News discovered Philip Peltz "once served a prison term for providing prostitutes to a federal employ," as the newspaper reported.

Poor Peltz, there he was trying to better himself, and they just wouldn't let him make an honest living.

Even those heartless editors down at the Post turned Peltz's stooge away. Why spend $100,000 on Berkowitz's own story when they already had printed it from start to finish. What else was there that David Berkowitz could tell us that we didn't already know?

All that was really left to learn about David Richard was whether he was competent to stand trial. And that decision was to be reached by Dr. David W. Schwartz, director of forensic psychiatry at Kings County. He was the alienist who in 1973 declared George Metesky, the Mad Bomber, cured and on his word freedom was granted the man who had terrorized New York for so many years.

Now Schwartz would probe the mind of another patient—the man who called himself Son of Sam, the .44-caliber killer.

CHAPTER XXII

HIS PADDED CELL

No sooner had David Berkowitz been issued his drab city hospital pajamas and put in a six-bed padded cell in solitary confinement than a wave of threats to kill the Son of Sam inundated the hospital. Authorities immediately installed an extraordinary guard in and outside the hospital and sealed off all entrances to protect some 6,000 patients and hospital staff.

Phones rang incessantly with calls from persons voicing intentions to take the life of the patient confined in the grim and spartan prison ward on the sixth floor of the hospital's G Building, at Winthrop Street and Albany Avenue.

But there were a few minor incidents. Five young men, for example, were seized near an entrance and detained for some hours by police. Someone had said they were friends of Stacy Moskowitz and had come to plant a bomb in Berkowitz's cell.

There was little fear, however, of harm being inflicted on the hospital's notorious patient—they don't call them prisoners there. Correction officers—a dozen strong on each of three shifts around the clock—were guarding David Berkowitz.

Once, only once, did the accused .44-caliber killer come close to being harmed. That happened on Sunday, August 28th, while Berkowitz was taking a shower. Carmelo Colon, an inmate who had been arrested for assault and committed for mental tests, noticed his slippers were missing. Something told him Berkowitz had taken them and he jumped David under the shower.

Correction officers moved in but Colon managed to deliver three or four punches to Berkowitz' head and body before he was pulled back.

Other than that, Berkowitz's stay was uneventful—except for a letter he received from his hero, Jimmy Breslin, who wrote that he wanted to see David. As Breslin put it:

"I said that in his letter to me last June he promised that he someday would introduce me to the person he calls Sam. I reminded him of the promise and said I wanted to come over and see him and meet Sam..."

The whole world had been introduced to Sam through David Berkowitz's confession—but Breslin was still looking for that intro.

Berkowitz' routine was monotonously the same for all the days and weeks he spent under observation at K.C.

In his private accommodation, separated from the other patients for his own protection, he could awaken what time he wanted and go to sleep when it pleased him. However there were hard and fast rules for meals. Breakfast was served at 8:15 a.m., lunch at noon, and dinner at 5:15 p.m.

Patients were permitted to use a dayroom which has TV and ping-pong, but Berkowitz wasn't granted that privilege because of his solitary confinement status.

He was also subjected to daily interviews with the psychiatrists. Usually two hours a day.

Tests were also administered in an effort to help reach a decision on whether he was capable of understanding the charges against him. One test involved tape recordings of conversations he had with doctors; by listening to these later rather than merely relying on notes, a doctor can make a better, more accurate determination. Berkowitz also was given formal psychological tests such as the personality profiles and ink blot interpretations. Then he also underwent physical testing to rule out the possibility of brain damage. Who knows whether that rock hurled at David when he was a kid and struck in the head didn't cause *whatever* inside his brain? These tests included brain wave scanning and others.

Berkowitz was allowed to read, but only a limited number of selected publications were allowed. No newspapers or magazines, no pornographic literature such as was strewn over his apartment floor for David while in the psychiatric lockup.

Of course there were visits from his father and his lawyers, the ones from Long Island, not Phil Peltz, whose efforts to hustle the tapes had gotten him hung up with every legal force from the Bar Association all the way up to the Appellate Division, the state's second highest court.

Justice Brown had made Peltz surrender the tapes to the court and prohibited him or anyone else from distributing any voice recordings of David Berkowitz.

Berkowitz also had more encounters with judges and courts in the time he was in Kings County. For the most part the proceedings were conducted in a makeshift courtroom—the recreation room in the prison ward at K.C. It was deemed safer to hold the hearings there than transport the patient to a courthouse.

On occasions when he was required to be in a courthouse, Berkowitz was convoyed like a shipment from the mint at Fort Knox. He was placed in a large prisoner van that the Department of Correction normally drives for a dozen or more persons; at least a dozen police cars and correction officers' vehicles were in the procession from the hospital and back. All the proceedings were mere formalities to satisfy the law insofar as Berkowitz's rights were concerned.

Because the Brooklyn detectives had busted the case Brooklyn had first crack at the prisoner—in the event he was found competent to stand trial. So Kings County District Attorney Eugene Gold went to the grand jury and obtained indictments in the killing of Stacy Moscowitz and blinding of Robert Violante.

He was asked how he felt when he learned David was arrested as Son of Sam.

"I cried," he answered.

There were others who were to cry now. They had shed tears when they lost loved ones to the .44-caliber killer's murderous bullets and had suffered at the side of those who did not die but will be maimed or scarred for the rest of their lives.

They were the parents and families and friends—and even the citizens of the city—who would not believe, didn't want to believe what was about to be heralded in court.

On Tuesday, August 23rd, Queens District Attorney John Santucci moved against Berkowitz with indictments for the murders of Christine Freund and Virginia Voskerichian and the wounding of Donna DeMasi, Joanne Lomino, Carl Denaro, Judy Placido, and Salvatore Lupo.

Next day, Bronx District Attorney Mario Merola's grand jury nailed the Son of Sam suspect for the .44-caliber murders of Valentina Suriani, Alexander Esau, and Donna Lauria, as well as the wounding of Jody Valente.

His first two arraignments in the hospital went off without any sign of abnormality or irrationality. But at the third, on Wednesday, August 24th, David Berkowitz pulled a shocker.

Swaying side to side as he stood before

Justice Alexander Chananau, the defendant was asked if he was David Berkowitz.

"Is that your name?" court clerk William Rinn asked.

"No, your honor, I am not," Berkowitz responded.

Lawyer Mark Heller scrambled to his feet and pleaded with Chananau: "Your honor, I request that no further questions be directed at the defendant and that he be allowed to stand mute.

Glaring at the defendant, the judge ordered: "Arraign the defendant!"

Berkowitz, who'd been given a haircut for this third court appearance, remained impassive for the balance of the proceeding.

Someone in the know said that Berkowitz's stunning response in court was not surprising because he had been going in and out of reality for all the time he'd been in his padded cell at K.C.

"There are times when he's alert and understands everything that's said to him. Other times, he's completely unaware of what's going on..."

Was David Berkowitz' behavior in court that day a precursor of what was yet to come when the psychiatric report was completed by Dr. Schwartz?

We'll soon see....

CHAPTER XXIII

A FATHER'S SORROW

The press room in the gleaming $18 million modern white-marbled State Supreme Court Building in Mineola was the setting for a most unusual encounter of reporters and the father of David Richard Berkowitz.

The short, balding white-haired man in the orange shirt and yellow windbreaker walked into the room squinting even with the dark glasses over his eyes.

The glare of television camera lights and the flash of photographers' strobes were blinding him.

Sixty-eight-year-old Nathan Berkowitz was escorted to the courthouse by Ira Jultak and Andrew Polin who had brought him over from their nearby law office. He shuffled into the room on legs that seemed almost ready to give out from under him.

Someone offered him a chair. He sat and immediately pulled a folded sheet that had been torn from a green stock stenographer's notepad. There was writing on the sheet. It was in longhand and had been penned with blue ink.

"I want to read something," he began. His voice trailed off for a moment. It was on the verge of breaking. He was choking on his sorrow.

"If David did these things," he began

falteringly, "I don't expect you to forgive him as this would be too much to ask of you.

"The only thing I do ask of you is to understand the pain and agony that is within me knowing the pain and agony of all you parents..." His voice cracked and he began to sob.

Jultak had told the reporters that Berkowitz had requested the press conference. He wanted to express his deep and heartfelt sympathy to all the parents and families of those killed, crippled and wounded by the .44-caliber killer. Because of failing health, Jultak and Polin had advised against that tactic. But Berkowitz insisted and even wrote the statement himself that he was now trying to deliver.

"Until a few days ago I was leading a normal-life in retirement, then my life was completely turned around. I keep thinking it is only a bad dream and that I would soon wake up. I don't know if what has been written about David is true or not. From what I read my mind cannot deny what my heart cannot accept." Again his voice cracked as he now was wracked by sobs.

"If what I read is true," he stammered again, "I would like to say to all those families, that have lost their children and have had children injured, I deeply grieve for you with all my heart.

"At this time, my loss is not because of one son that I adopted, but my loss is multiplied by what each and every one of the parents of these crimes feels in his or her heart.

"I ask of all of you not to burden us with your feelings towards David. By us, I mean all those people who have known David and me. We too are victims of this tragedy.

"I will live with this heartache for the rest of my life. I am so deeply saddened that nothing I can say can really express my deep sorrow for all of you parents.

"Thank you for listening to me—my prayers will be with you all."

Reporters's voices rose in a cacaphonous drone.

"What kind of a boy was David?"

"When did you last see your son?"

The father answered, "Last Summer."

"What was your reaction when you first heard about the .44-caliber killings?"

Berkowitz shook his head. "That it was some kind of nut."

CHAPTER XXIV

THE SCALES OF JUSTICE

The psychiatric report prepared by Dr. Schwartz and a colleague, Dr. Richard L. Weidenbacher Jr., was brought to Justice Gerald S. Held.

"This report was delivered in this envelope," the judge said in the packed courtroom. "I am now going to open it for the first time.

"I say this because there have been reports in the media concerning the bottom line of this report. No one in this courtroom, as far as I know, knows what the report contains. I am now going to open it and break the seal.

"I am now going to hand it to defense counsel and the district attorney."

The lawyers took their copies and retired to private rooms to read and digest the findings. An hour later they were back in court.

Justice Held then read from the ten-page report, but he did not read it in its entirety; merely two pages while the other eight were ordered sealed.

The bottom line was that:

"It is the opinion of each of us that the defendant is an incapacitated person, as a result of mental disease or defect, lacks capacity to understand the proceeding against him or to assist in his own defense. The details of our report are as follows:

"1. Diagnosis: Paranoia

"2. Prognosis: Guarded

"3. Nature and extent of examination: The patient was examined psychiatrically on August 12, 13, and 14 (Dr. Schwartz), August 17 (Dr. Weidenbacher), and August 18 and 22 (both examiners) for a total of approximately 11 hours."

The psychiatrists also reported that they conferred at length with Berkowitz's father and studied the various letters he had written to his father, as well as the notes to Captain Borrelli, to Breslin and the threatening notes to Sam Carr.

District Attorney Gold moved immediately to have a psychiatrist of his choosing examine the defendant.

"It is entirely possible that David Berkowitz is suffering from paranoia," said Gold, "but it is also possible that this illness which is characterized by delusions such as persecution or grandeur, do not make him incompetent to stand trial..."

The court granted Gold's application for such an examination and ordered a hearing in the same court for the early Fall.

Gold was later joined in that motion by Prosecutors Santucci and Merola.

The psychiatric findings generated a shockwave among the survivors and families of the victims.

From his Kings County Hospital bed, Robert Violante, now beginning to get a partial restoration of his sight in his right eye, called the report "a copout....the law had better wake up and do its job," he said.

Christine Freund's mother: "I think he is not crazy. He deserves to be punished. He is not stupid, believe me. He knows what he was doing. He was able to work at the post office; earn his money. He could talk about the killings with people and never give himself away. Yes, I say punish him—he deserves it."

John Diel who was going to marry Miss Freund was furious. "Psychiatrists? What they did here is a farce. Bartenders know more than they do," said the man who is one. "This guy is on a vacation now. Good food, exercise, TV. All through his life he was a loser. All he had was a stinking little apartment and his .44. Now he's got it made. What else could he want?"

Rose Lauria who lost her only daughter in the .44-caliber killer's first foray, was devastated by the news in court. "He knew what he was doing. No dog told him to do that..."

Another mother who lived a few blocks away and whose daughter Jody Valente was wounded in that attack said: "They've got to be kidding, those doctors. With what he did? The misery and anxiety he caused us all? No, I don't think he's insane. He planned everything he did. And he should be tried for it."

Yolanda Voskerichian echoed the same frustrations felt by the other mothers. "I'm terribly sad for what happened to us. But we don't have anything to say about it now. It's

318

up to the people with power. For me, I think he has to be on trial. We are the ones affected, but we have no power to put him on trial."

Rosemary Keenan, the detective's daughter who escaped harm when her date, Carl Denaro, was shot, couldn't believe what Dr. Schwartz and Dr. Weidenbacher came up with. "What good does it do what I say? They won't change their decision because of what the victims think. Of course I think he should stand trial. But if they put him away in a mental institution what guarantee is there they won't say he's okay in a few months or years and let him out."

DeNaro, who walks around with a steel plate in his head as a result of the wound inflicted by the .44-caliber killer, wasn't as concerned as the others about the findings so long as the man wasn't freed. "A lay person can't really say what they've decided is wrong. I don't care if, after a trial, he goes to jail or spends the rest of his life in a mental institution. But I can't see how he could possibly walk the streets again in seven or eight years. It wouldn't be like releasing an 80-year old who couldn't harm anyone. He'd still be young. That would be a terrible thing."

Neysa Moskowitz was disgusted with the finding but hopeful that the new examination ordered by Justice Held may bring a different result. "I'll have no faith in the court system," she said, "if Berkowitz is again found incompetent.

319

Charles Lomino, whose daughter Joanne is paralyzed from the waist down, echoed Mrs. Moskowitz' hope. "This is not yet the end...."

*   *   *

No, it isn't the end. Not after David Richard Berkowitz, in what certainly must have been one of his more lucid moments in his padded cell responded to Jimmy Breslin's letter asking to chat.

"Dear Mr. Breslin,

"It has come to my attention that you wish to speak with me. Well, all you have to do is come over to my home at Kings County Hospital. At this time I am unable to visit you.

"I am quite disgusted with the way the Press has been spreading lies about me but perhaps some of these can be ironed out in our meeting. However, I am not one to cry out a case of injustice.

"I hope Mayor Beame enjoys dribbling my head across the court. This is really [crossed out] like a circus event with clowns and animals. Please bring a beer when you come.

"Sincerely
"David Berkowitz"

No, it certainly couldn't be the end. Not after that letter...